Your S

Trust the Whisper
Of Your Soul

JohnA Passaro

Every Breath Is Gold
Memoir Series
Book 3

YOUR SOUL KNOWS

Text copyright ©

2015 JohnA Passaro

ISBN/EAN 13:/ 978-1511540759
ISBN-10: 1511540753
ASIN - B00VGLVOXO

Your Soul Knows ppb 6x9 20180802

All Rights Reserved

Any reproduction of this material by any means,
In whole or in part,
Needs expressed written consent of its author

Life is a school,
Where you learn to remember
What your soul already knows.

Caroline Myss

For All Books by JohnA Passaro

Go to:

www.johnapassaroblog.com/books

TABLE OF CONTENTS

1. iFight — 7
2. I'm Fine — 14
3. Open Your Gifts — 16
4. Breadcrumbs and Time — 20
5. Timeless — 28
6. Delayed Divine Explanation — 32
7. The Full Picture — 35
8. X-Ray — 38
9. September 12th — 45
10. Listen, Trust, Act — 51
11. More Love — 78
12. I Hear You — 81
13. The Jungle — 83
14. Mr. Duplicity — 85
15. The Formula — 88
16. Earn Your Way — 92
17. A Stretch and a Smile — 97
18. What I Know For Sure — 101
19. #119,104 — 103
20. Runny Knows — 105
21. Snorkeling — 109
22. Averting a Crash — 115
23. The Fight of Your Life — 117
24. A Dark Night of the Soul — 120
25. Don't Eat My Food — 130
26. 3 A.M. Emails — 136
27. Thumper — 143
28. Bless You — 149
29. The Voice — 153
30. The Forest For the Trees — 155

-1-
IFIGHT

If I lay here,
Would you lay with me
And just look at the world?

Chasing Cars

September 19th, 2014

I am standing in line outside of an AT&T store on an abnormally cold September morning. I am waiting for the privilege to be one of the first people on earth, to be able to purchase Apples' new iPhone 6 Plus.

I had always promised myself I would never be *that* person camping out for a new release, but today it was what I needed to do.

Today, standing in line in the bitter cold, was actually the best use of my time.

When I awoke this morning, I realized somehow, someway, I hadn't left my house in over twenty days; a combination stemming from working from home and being a caregiver to my daughter Jess.

Standing in line in the freezing cold, with a brisk wind blowing in my face is better than the alternative, another day inside, sheltered from the elements.
So here I am, some eighteen people deep standing in line.

Every twenty minutes or so, an AT&T representative braves the cold, opens the door and to magnify the experience, lets one shopper into the store at a time.

The round trip shopping experience takes approximately twenty minutes. To the people standing outside in the cold, it seems much longer.

Based on where I am in line, I figure I have at least another four-hour wait ahead of me.

Just after letting in the latest shopper, the AT&T spokesperson leaves the warmth and shelter of the store, steps outside and makes two announcements.

His first announcement is, due to short supply, the store is limiting each person to only one new iPhone purchase or upgrade, per visit, today.

I am here to upgrade five iPhones.

I am informed to accomplish my task, I will need to stand in line a total of five different times today.

The second announcement the AT&T representative makes is designed to prevent people from waiting in line for naught. He informs the crowd he is no longer allowing any new people to get online, as he believes the store's supply of new iPhones will soon be exhausted.

Upon hearing these two new announcements, a Hispanic lady about five people deep in line takes out her "outdated" iPhone and makes a phone call to her family – she asks them to come down to the store, as they need to be present to get their new iPhone.

In a few short minutes, six of her relatives get to the store and attempt to merge into the line where she is standing.

The last six people on the end of the line suddenly realize their chances of getting a new iPhone today are now in jeopardy because of this new "merger." They vocally express their displeasure to the AT&T employee, who has sheltered himself from both the cold and the crowd by retreating inside the store behind a glass door.

The AT&T employee initially makes believe that he cannot hear the concerns of the people on the back of the line. He acts as if the glass door that separates them is soundproof and he lets their discontent go unacknowledged.

He stands behind the glass door with a blank stare, hoping the crowd's outcry will subside on its own.

It does not.

It escalates.

Within minutes, the situation erupts when the people who are standing in the back of the line, storm the front of the line, demanding fairness.

This new turn of events irritates the people who are standing in the middle of the line and they, too, decide to voice their displeasure and head towards the front of the line with the same concern.

Now there is no line, just a mass of disorderly people who feel slighted, all hovering near the front of the line.

The Hispanic lady is now verbally abused by nearly everyone in the line.

It's getting ugly.

The Hispanic lady makes a conscious decision that the best defense is always a good offense and she starts to verbally abuse her abusers.
Within seconds, people are in each other's faces and personal spaces.

Somehow, the verbal abuse turns racial.

The AT&T rep, who now seems annoyed that his strategy of ignoring the concerns of the crowd did not work, leaves his post at the door and goes to get help.

By the time he gets back a minute later, the mass of people outside the glass door are nearly brawling.

All over an iPhone.

Actually, all over an upgrade of an iPhone.

Ironically, all over an upgrade with a feature that was designed to make it easier for people to communicate with one another.

You can't make this stuff up.
I am standing back where the line once was, taking in the absolute absurdity of the situation.

I just want to walk up to the front of the line and scream:

"What the heck are you fighting for - it is a phone!"

But I remain quiet instead.

Eventually, the AT&T store rep calms everyone down by negotiating an agreement between the two sides.

He decides he will allow the six new people who merged into the line to enter the store with the Hispanic lady but they will not be able to purchase a phone themselves unless they go to the end of the line.

All parties agree this is fair.

The newly formed group enters the store together, and twenty minutes later, all seven of them are carrying an AT&T bag with their new iPhones inside.

As they exit the store, all seven of them taunt the crowd by waiving their bags high in the air.

A brawl nearly breaks out.

The only thing that saves the situation from erupting into a physical altercation is that the seven new owners of the iPhone 6 Plus jump into their car, which is parked nearby.

As soon as they get to safety inside the vehicle, their urge to taunt the people who are standing in line re-emerges.

They quickly close and lock the doors, roll down the windows and then they slowly drive the car by the crowd, while simultaneously giving everyone in line the middle finger.

A person from the line, who is infuriated with the whole situation, suddenly starts chasing after the vehicle while yelling racial slurs.

Thankfully, the car speeds away without altercation.

I contemplate how disturbing it is that people would treat each other so horribly, all over an upgrade of a phone. Certainly, this is not what Steve Jobs had in mind when he set out to change the world.

A second thought comes to my mind that five years ago I probably would have been one of these people iFighting over an iPhone.

But not today.

Today, I see life differently.

I have adversity to thank for that.

After another few hours of waiting in line, it is finally my turn to shop.

As I am about to enter the store the AT&T worker politely puts his forearm in front of my chest stopping me in my tracks and says,

"I am sorry - we are currently out of the iPhone 6 Plus."

Reflexively, my blood starts to boil.

I breathe deeply, and I exhale.

At this time I know I have a choice to make.
I could let standing in line for the last four hours in the blistering cold ruin my day, which would assuredly cause a negative ripple effect throughout the lives of anyone with whom I come in contact, which would then cause them to set off their own tsunami of negativity, or I can have some perspective.

I decide to have some perspective.

A quote by Victor Frankl comes to my mind:

"Between stimulus and response, there is a space.
In that space lies our freedom and our power to choose our response.
In our response lies our growth and our happiness."

Today, I decide to grow and to be happy.

I have adversity to thank for that.

Adversity has taught me what matters in life and what does not.

It has given me a new perspective; one I would not trade for anything in the world, except Jess's recovery.

I ask the AT&T worker when he expects more iPhone 6 Plus's to arrive.
He responds that he doesn't expect any more to come in for at least another six weeks.

I say, "Thank you very much, have a great day," and I head back home.

Like I said before, I have learned what is important in life.

Being a "Life Changing Events Club Member" has taught me that I can use my iPhone 5s, with my 4.4-inch screen, for another six weeks.
It's not going to kill me.

I have learned to save my fight for battles that are important in my life.

I fight every day, not for an iPhone, but for life, for love, for meaning and for the trust and courage to listen to my soul.

That is worth fighting for.

- 2 -
I'M FINE

I'm
Sad
Hurt
Vulnerable
Lost
Heart Broken
Dying inside
Fine

As I am walking to my vehicle, I run into an old friend, one whom I have not seen in many years.

In my mind, I try to decipher whether the last time I have seen him was "BJ" or "AJ," Before Jess or After Jess.

That is how I view my life now.

As I am working on solving this chronological puzzle, my old friend asks me: "John, how *are* you?" and when he emphasizes the word *are* a second longer than most people would, the circumstances of when the last time I had last seen my friend come to the forefront of my mind.
The last time, come to think of it, was at the gas station pumping gas immediately after I left the hospital for the first time in over four days when Jess was originally admitted back in 2009.

So, the answer is "AJ" - After Jess.

I was an emotional zombie at that time.

Today, I am only 49% zombie.

It has taken me over five years to recapture 51% of my life.

It has been one of the hardest things I have ever had to do, but I have done it.

I refocus on his question.

I don't know how to answer his question of "How *are* you?"

Is it a nicety, or does he really want to know?

I finally answer, "I am fine," we exchange a few niceties, and I head to my truck.

Just before I get to my truck, I have this urge to turn around and to go back and say to my old friend:

"You know, I'm not fine.
I'm far from ok.
I'm barely hanging on.
I'm fighting every day to just be ok.

That's how I am if you really want to know.

How are you?"

But instead, I put the key in the ignition, and I drive away.

At this point in my life, I am many things, but "fine" is still not one of them.

- 3 -
OPEN YOUR GIFTS

Every adversity,
Every failure,
Every heartache,
Carries with it
The seed of something greater.

Napoleon Hill
Think and Grow Rich

A little more than five years ago my world was knocked off of its axis and out of its orbit when my daughter Jessica lost oxygen to her brain for six minutes.

Every second of every day since that derailment, I have been trying to get my life back onto its orbit.

It is sort of like attempting to get back on a fast-moving merry-go-round, but every time I try, my life just spits me right back out.

With each failed attempt to regain my orbit, I learn a little more about the universe.

Recently, I have learned according to the Universal Law of "The Seed of Something Greater," when the universe takes something from you it is required to give you 'The Seed of Something Greater' in return.

What you do with that seed, whether you plant and nourish it and let it grow to bear fruit, or whether you ignore it and let it wither and die, is up to you.

The seed is simple and complex at the same time.

It is a powerful gift.

One, which is comprised of many truths.

One of those truths is perspective.

Perspective is like viewing a high definition television for the first time, it crystallizes the beauty and the details of life.

Perspective allows you to see life using the same set of eyes, but it enables you to see things you previously overlooked, things that were hiding in plain sight.

Perspective allows you to view life differently.

Perspective allows you to live your life exponentially better by experiencing every aspect of your life more magnificently.

Perspective hasn't made my loss any less painful, but it has given me clarity on what is truly important in life.

To treat one another with love.

That is it.

Devon Franklin, in his book "Produced by Faith," writes:
"The truth is, you and I are in control of only two things:

How we prepare for what might happen and how we respond to what just happened."

I believe there is a third thing we are in control of – the ability to treat each other with love.

That, we all can do.

And it is there where we should concentrate all of our energies.

To treat each other with love doesn't require money, or social status or education; it only requires we open the gifts we each have received from having adversity in our lives.

To have perspective.

Adversity is a very valuable resource.

I recently heard someone speak about a phenomenon in our generation, one where some well-meaning parents try to clear the path for their children by eliminating all adversity in their lives, they called it Genetically Modified Parenting.

It is sort of like what Monsanto is doing to corn.

Monsanto, by genetically modifying the DNA of corn, allows more corn to be produced, but in the process sucks the nutritional value out of the corn, which defeats the point of producing corn.

In essence, this phenomenon of parents eliminating adversity from their kids' lives is producing genetically modified kids.

By eliminating adversity in their kid's lives, these parents have sucked the nutrition out of their kids' lives.
Adversity is the nutrition, which spurs growth.

Ironically, these well-meaning parents have done the exact opposite of what they intended to do.

They are eliminating the one thing that will provide their kids with more growth – adversity.

Adversity is a gift.

It is a rare person in this world who understands this truth before adversity strikes them.

For the rest of us, it requires a life-changing event to fully comprehend the value of adversity.

I know there is more than enough adversity in this world, which conversely should mean there should be more than enough perspective in this world as well.

There is not.

The world's most valuable, untapped natural resources are the gifts that have been earned through adversity and have yet to be opened - seed's that can wither away or bear fruit.

Imagine how different this world would be if everyone opened their gift and gained perspective.
I just wrote that to myself on my outdated iPhone 5s.

And it didn't kill me.

- 4 -
BREADCRUMBS AND TIME

Character cannot be developed in ease and quiet.
Only through experience of trial and suffering
Can the soul be strengthened.
Vision cleared,
Ambition inspired,
And success achieved.

Helen Keller

October 17th, 2014

No matter how many times I witness it, it never gets easier.

The sight of Jessie being put on a gurney and carried out of the house and into an ambulance nearly breaks me every time.

Today's episode is only a minor crisis, one where Jess's feeding tube needs to be replaced due to a slight pinhole, which at this time is not an emergency, but BettyJane and I have learned to nip things in the bud before they turn into a full-blown crisis.

Over the last six months, BettyJane and I have been very fortunate, as Jess has not needed a hospital stay, and for that, we are very grateful.

But our new normal has posed new problems, which we both strive to overcome with each new day.

BettyJane and I are getting accustomed to expecting the expected, and the unexpected, both at the same time.

Handling a new crisis with each new day has just become our new normal.

Chaos has snaked itself into our daily lives.

We have learned to handle it well.

It is amazing, a crisis, which used to wipe us out for six weeks, is now only a blip on our caregivers' radar.

Our ability to handle the unexpected has become a very valuable tool, but something neither BettyJane nor I, deem as any badge of honor.

Together, we have learned the difference between what is important in life and what is just plain noise, designed to distract us from accomplishing our mission.

We have learned to concentrate on what is important and to ignore the noise.
That sounds simple, but it is not.

BettyJane and I have weathered an unrelenting emotional storm that has made us feel alone, together, if that makes any sense.

It has been during this pelting storm I have come to realize everyone on this earth ultimately has the same goals in life, and that is to be happy, to find meaning in their life, to know they mattered, that they made a difference in their world.

What makes one happy, and how one finds meaning in their life, is what makes us all different.

We are all the same, but different.

We are all on our unique journey, intertwined and connected, made whole through love.

With BettyJane, on her way to the emergency room with Jess, and both Maverick and Travis away at college and Cassidy in school, this is the first time in over five years I am alone in my own home.

I don't mean the feeling of being alone; I mean the actual physicality of being alone.

I look around my house.

I am currently the best version of myself I have ever been, yet at times, I fear that may not be good enough.

I wonder what is going to happen to my family over the next six years.

It is as if life knows I am willing to pay any price to fix my life and with each new day it keeps upping the ante.

No matter how exorbitant the price, life knows I will pay it.

And I do.
Each day.

By the end of the day both BettyJane and I are depleted of all of our life currency, but somehow by the time the sun rises anew, we miraculously find more change in the proverbial cushions of our life's couch.

Each day we come up with the increased ante for entrance into a new day, and on the days we either can't come up with the increased ante, or we just don't want too, the ante miraculously appears.

In Victor Frankl's book, "A Mans Search For Meaning" he writes:

"Yes, a man can get used to anything, but do not ask us how."
How BettyJane and I have made it this far, I do not know.

But I do know we fight every day to not get used to our situation.

I look around.

Everything in this house is so still.

So much has happened here.

So little is happening here.

I have been so patient; I have recently become impatient with being patient.

The years are flying by, yet one night of caregiving seems like an eternity.
One half of me is a total mess, while the other half is extraordinarily sharp.

My mind races, yet my body is still.

I'm in love with life, yet I wouldn't want anyone alive to ever live through my experiences.

I dread my circumstances.

I have been walking on the edge for so long that the view of the abyss is no longer scary.

I tightrope over the abyss every day without ever looking down. My fear is one day I will look down, just for a second and lose my balance. I know just one misstep could be devastating to my family.

Therefore, to make sure that never happens, I overcompensate by looking up a little more than I should.

I'd rather be a little Pollyanna than fall into the black hole of despair.

I look for meaning in everything, yet at times everything seems so void of any meaning at all.

At times I feel there is no meaning worth all of this suffering and I silently curse the lessons the universe may be in the process of trying to teach me.

At other times I am curious to learn what lessons can be worth all of this pain and suffering.

I look forward to its magnificence and splendor when all of the moving parts come together, and the master plan is eventually revealed to me.

I can't help thinking how cruel it is to have to exchange pain and suffering for universal meaning in life.

I can't help thinking if I were the head of the universe I wouldn't teach this way – through pain and suffering.

Why does it have to be that way?

What do you do when your belief and your threshold for pain have both reached their maximum capacity?

Which one will win out?

How do I beat this?

What is the plan?

I feel like I am losing…

I need to win.

This is just five minutes inside my head.

Constant.
Intense.
Looping.
Non-Stop.

I need to matter.

I need to make a difference in my world.
I need to win.

For Jess.

For my family.

For me.

It is at times like these I think about a rewind button for life.

If I could only rewind the world to August 21st, 2009, 9:00 pm and press stop.

The end.

Never to hit play again.

No need to go any further than that.

No eternal pain, no great sadness, no feeling of having no impact.

If you were to give me a choice of only living up to that exact time, a second before "Before Jess" turned into "After Jess," 99% of me would sign on the dotted line.

But there is 1% of me that wants to continue on my unique journey in this living hell for the sole reason of gaining a greater understanding of the universe, and the universal law that states with every adversity there is a potential seed of something greater.

That 1% of me is ultra curious as to what that something greater is.

It must be magnificent.

To quote Barbara Brown Taylor:

"The places I least want to go are the riches places. The richest treasure is hidden there."

I need to find that treasure.

I need to share that treasure.

I need to find and plant that seed.
I am a competitor by nature and if I stop without finding and planting that seed that would mean that I would lose.

So for me to win, I must weather the storm and then find and plant the seed of a greater good.

I believe if I can do that, I will win this fight.

I so strive for meaning in everything.

There has to be a reason, a meaning, a lesson.

There has to be something more than the loss, the suffering, and the helplessness.

There has to be something greater.

Logically, that something greater should be the feeling of love and enlightenment and the sense of knowing.

As much as my mind wants to rewind back to the day and time when my daughter's life changed, there is something that tells me to proceed.

To find the gift of a greater good.

To open it.

To plant the seed.

To share it with the world.

So I do.

- 5 -
TIMELESS

To stand on the meeting of two eternities,
The past and the future
Which is precisely the current moment.

Henry David Thoreau

I enter my kitchen in my empty house.

I take out my outdated iPhone, and I start to reminisce by reading a copy of a letter I had written to my mom during my freshmen year in college some years ago. I found this letter sitting on my mom's counter when I visited her, the other day.

As I am reading my own words off the wrinkled yellowing pages, a few thoughts come to mind.

The first thought is how much has changed over those thirty-one years.

A handwritten letter sent through the mail.

Think of that.

Actually putting pen to paper, with your own handwriting, placing that communication in the mail and within three days having it arrive at the intended destination.
Just think of how much life has sped up.

Now that same letter can be sent within a few seconds to its target by electronic mail.

We now live at the speed of light instead of the speed of life.

The second thing that strikes me is the creased, wrinkled, yellowing paper.

Obviously, the letter was folded, put in an envelope and sent through the mail. When the envelope was opened, and the letter was taken out of the envelope, the creases never went away. Along the creases, the paper became worn and thin, and that is where the yellowing was most distinct. The creases, wrinkles, and yellowing are the universe's way of authenticating the age of the letter.

The letter has withstood the test of time.

And so has its message.

As I read the letter, I start to realize how much has not changed with time.

You see, I wrote this letter some thirty-one years ago to inform my mom I no longer had the desire to wrestle in college.

That I had lost the desire to compete, and I thought wrestling was a dead end for me.

My main reason was I no longer had a big goal.

I felt the sacrifices I would have to make seemed greater than the prize I would receive.

And just like that, I stopped.

The switch was turned off.

In the rest of the letter, I wrote about appreciation and my lack of communication.

I let my mom know how much I appreciated all she did to support me during my wrestling career, under some tough financial times. And how sorry I was for never letting her or my father know they were great people. And I really felt bad for never communicating that to them during my now seemingly selfish pursuit of wrestling glory.

This part of the letter confirmed two things to me: one, the importance of having big goals, and two, the importance of communicating one's appreciation.

When one does not have big goals, the journey and the price one has to pay will not seem worth it, and slowly but surely one's goals will turn to dreams, one's dreams will turn to wishes, and one's wishes will turn to dust.

Just like that.

I want the exact opposite.

I fight every day to hold onto the big goal of Jess's recovery.

I want what Will McDonough of the Iowa Hawkeyes talks about when he says:
"That my dreams became my vision. My vision became my reality."
I want to go in that direction.

I have to hold on to my pursuit of a big goal with Jess. I have to believe the price I am paying is going to be worth it in the end.

I have to believe there is a greater good.

I have to find that seed.

As far as the communication part of the letter, I envisioned myself nearing the tail end of my life, rummaging through a box of valuable items I had saved throughout my life. And coming across a wrinkled, yellowing, handwritten letter from my child who let me know how much they appreciated everything I did for them, and how that would make me feel.
And I smile.

I smile because I envision that future letter is signed by Jess.

I smile because I am positive that my mom felt the same way when she first read the letter I had sent to her.

I held on to the thought that one of my mom's most valuable possessions in her life was a letter from me letting her know I appreciated her and the way she brought me up, that she mattered and made a difference in my world.

And that was a great feeling.

It has endured the test of time.

I am going to put a copy of the letter I sent to my mom, some thirty-one years ago, in my own box of my life's most valuable items.

- 6 -
DELAYED DIVINE EXPLANATION

There are divine reasons
For what happened in the past.
I don't know those reasons
But I investigate them
And I try to figure them out.

Tom Brands

I have such a box.

A box in which I have kept my life's memories.

Throughout my whole life, whenever I experienced an important event, I would always place something from that event into my box.

Whether it was a ticket stub from a playoff game, or a business card from a new job, or just a picture of family and friends getting together, I saved each memory in my box.

This box became the breadcrumb trail of my life, mapping out the weird and windy road my life is on.
I have had this box for as long as I can remember.

Around the time cameras started to appear on every cell phone, I stopped adding items to my box, as technology turned my box into the audio cassette tape in an mp3 world.

When that technological advancement occurred, saving memories on my cell phone became a much more convenient way of archiving my life.

I forgot about my box for many years.

But today it is on my mind, as I would like to add a copy of this letter I wrote to my mom to it.

Even though I have not seen my box for many years, I know exactly where it is - top shelf, left-hand side of my bedroom closet.

I go to its location.

It is sitting there looking at me, almost saying to me, "What took you so long to get here?"

I hesitate.

I hesitate because I know, as soon as I open my box, my "BJ," Before Jess, life will reemerge.

And I don't know if I can handle that at this time.

Dante wrote: *"There is no greater sorrow than to recall in misery the time when we were happy."*

I decide to proceed anyway.

I reach up, and I am very careful in my attempt to bring my box down from the top shelf.

The box is overflowing to the point where the cover of the box is acting more like a top to a pile of papers, rather than acting like an actual cover that encapsulates and protects the contents of the box.

As I bring the box down from the top shelf, I attempt to balance the huge pile of memories, but I fail to do so. The box tips over and all the memories of my entire life scatter all over the floor.

I sit stunned for a few seconds, and then I start to collect the spilled contents to put them back into my box.

With each item that I collected, I found new meaning to some of the events that happened in my life.

And some of the pieces of the jig-saw puzzle titled, "JohnA Passaro" started to come together to form the picture of my life.

- 7 -
THE FULL PICTURE

All endings
Are also beginnings.
We just don't know it
At the time.

Mitch Albom
The Five People That You Meet In Heaven

The very first item I pick up off of the floor is a St. Louis Post-Dispatch newspaper; dated September 28, 1998.

The newspapers front-page headline has Mark McGwire pumping his fist rounding first base while celebrating his historic 70th home run during the seemingly magnificent 1998 Major League Baseball season.

Up until that point, that was the single greatest sports achievement I had ever witnessed in my life.

It is amazing how time, when viewed in retrospect, provides a totally different perspective.
What I once thought was the single greatest achievement in the history of baseball, turned out to be, with time, a fraudulent, meaningless event.

An event that was so real in my mind's eye, time has exposed it to be a fake, a fraud.

Mark McGwire's historic record-breaking performance in 1998 will forever be tainted by the suspicion that he used performance-enhancing drugs to accomplish it.

Within just a few years of his achievement, McGwire traded the flashes of the fans cameras taking pictures of him triumphantly rounding the bases after hitting his 70th home run of that season, for those of the press's glaring snapshots of him unceremoniously pleading the 5th Amendment during a Congressional Hearing into performance-enhancing drugs in Major League Baseball.

Looking back, Mark McGwire's 1998 baseball season has taught me the importance of letting the full picture develop.

Life is more like a Polaroid camera than a digital camera.

I have learned the full picture of ones' life does not develop instantaneously, but rather it develops slowly, over time.

In the past, before the digital camera was invented, one would click a button on the Polaroid camera, and a picture would shoot out, a picture that would develop in a few minutes.

I have learned life is the same way, except minutes are replaced by years.

Mark McGwire's fall from grace was unimaginable to me at the time.

An absolutely spectacular event has, with time, proven to be totally meaningless.

And that makes me think.

Maybe, just maybe, according to "The Universal Law of Opposites," the inverse can also be true.

Maybe, time will reveal that horrific events, ones that seem totally void of any meaning, will eventually reveal real significance, great purpose and will prove to have the most meaning in our lives.

I believe that.

Sometimes, we just need to allow the full picture to develop.

- 8 -
X-Ray

What I am looking for,
Is not out there
It is within me.

Helen Keller

The second item that I pick up off of the floor is an X-Ray of my daughter Jessica's chest, from when she was two years old.

I don't have to hold the X-Ray up to the light; I know what it would show.

It would show me everything that we need in life is already inside of us.

Jessica was our first-born.

BettyJane and I were newbies as parents.

At the time, we thought we did a good job of childproofing our home.

Early in our parenting life, we learned that we were wrong.
We had no idea we had to nail down everything in our house or else it would end up in Jess's mouth.
During the Christmas season in 1992, when she was a two-year-old toddler, Jess was left unsupervised for just a few seconds, which

was just enough time for her to find her way to the nativity set we had on the floor next to our Christmas tree.

Immediately, BettyJane and I ran to grab Jess away from the Christmas tree. We feared she might grab onto a branch, which would then cause the huge tree to come tumbling down on top of her.

Thankfully, we got to Jess just as she was reaching up, to pull down on a branch.

Our first reaction was a momentary sense of pride as we thought we had just saved Jess from danger, a feeling we falsely extrapolated into the assumption that we would always be there for Jess, keeping her safe from any and all looming dangers in the future.

Like I said, we were newbie parents.

As I held Jess in my arms after saving her from herself, I pushed Jess's hand away from her mouth, and that is when I noticed that the manger in the nativity set on the floor near the Christmas tree was empty.

The one-inch baby Jesus Christmas ornament was gone.

BettyJane and I immediately searched everywhere for the missing Christmas ornament.

We could not find it anywhere.

There was only one logical explanation. Jessica must have put it into her mouth before we got to her and she must have swallowed it.

Frantically, BettyJane and I made our first trip to the ER as parents that night.

After an X-Ray and a three-hour wait, our parental suspicions were confirmed.

As soon as the doctor put the picture of Jess's chest up on the X-Ray board and turned on the backlight, the mystery of the missing baby Jesus was solved.

There, dead center in Jess's chest was the ornament of the baby Jesus.

But a funny thing happened when Jess swallowed the ornament.

The ornament went down Jess's windpipe like a person going down a water ride, thus making the baby Jesus ornament look more like a mature Jesus, one with outstretched arms instead of an infant lying in a manger.
When we looked at the X-ray, it looked like an adult Jesus was blessing baby Jessica from inside her own body.

I remember asking the doctor for a copy of the X-ray, as the image was spectacular.

He obliged.

Along with a copy of the X-Ray, the doctor gave BettyJane and I a game plan on how we were going to handle the extraction of the ornament from Jess's tiny two-year-old body.

The ER doctor said the ornament should pass naturally through Jess's system within 24 hours.
He said it was very important we checked Jess's stool over the next day, to make sure she successfully passed it through her system.

"If it passes, she will be fine," the doctor said.

If it did not, or if the ornament somehow got lodged in Jess's intestine, we were to bring Jess back to the ER immediately. The doctor stressed to both BettyJane and I to make sure we inspected Jessica's stool each time she pooped to make sure the ornament passed safely through her system.

That sounded simple enough.

It was not.

The next day we were scheduled to travel to Florida, by plane.

It just so happened Jess's next poop was aboard that plane ride.

I remember on that flight, BettyJane, with the dirty diaper in hand, casually walking up to a stewardess and asking her for a fork.

The look on the stewardess's face was priceless.

Aghast, the stewardess handed BettyJane a plastic fork and blankly stared at her as she walked towards the bathroom, where she was off to rummage through Jess's dirty diaper to make sure the ornament passed through Jess's system.

I remember the same stewardess's jaw drop when BettyJane ran out of the bathroom a few minutes later excitedly yelling,

"I got it!"

"I got it!"
While she still had the fork in one hand and the dirty diaper in the other.

Jess had passed the baby Jesus ornament on her first attempt.

We were so proud.

It has been twenty-two years since I had last seen this X-Ray. I remember it like it was yesterday.

Seeing this X-ray brings a smile to my face and a realization to my mind.

My mind fast-forwards to a conversation I had with Jess when she was nineteen years old, a few days before she would lose oxygen to her brain for six minutes.

She had asked me if I believed in God.

It was a rather odd question as Jess, and I never talked about such things.

I told her I did believe in God.

I could see her struggling with her own belief when she asked me:

"If there is a God, then why does he let bad things happen?"

I told her I didn't have an answer to that, I had often wondered that myself.

Jess then asked me if I believed in the details of our religion and I gave her this advice:

"Jess, God is love, everyone believes in love.
Just follow the love that is inside you, Jess, and you will always be okay."

That statement turned out to be prophetic advice in reverse, as the Love was literally inside of Jess at the age of two.

I am looking at the X-Ray that proves it.

Just a few days after giving Jessica the advice, *"To follow the Love that was inside of her,"* Jess lost oxygen to her brain for six minutes. She was put into a medically induced coma to allow her brain to heal.

Jess has since slowly started to heal.

It has been just over five years.

She fights every day to regain her cognitive functions.

It is a struggle that is so heart wrenching to watch, and one that requires a deep faith to continue to conquer.

"Just follow the Love that is inside of you, Jess."

I know I do every day.

Seeing this X-ray reminds me that everything that we need to get through any adversity in life is already inside of us.

Why do bad things happen in life?

I don't know.

But I do know that time can give one a new perspective.

Mark McGwire proved that something that was so awesome to watch take place daily, eventually, with time, proved to be so meaningless.

Every day of my life I am trying to prove the inverse – that something that is so heartbreaking to watch daily will one day prove to be full of meaning and purpose.

I believe that.

I believe when bad things happen to good people it is for a greater good, a bigger picture.

A picture that just takes time to fully develop.

I believe when that picture does fully develop, it will be as clear as crystal, as meaningful as the universe and as revealing as an X-ray.

- 9 -
SEPTEMBER 12TH

There are some experiences in life
They haven't invented the right words for.

Lisa Kleypas
Married by Morning

I pick up an old piece of paper off of the floor.

Its edges are frayed and discolored.

The paper is a rejection notice I received from a job interview some twenty-two years ago.

It reads:

Dear Mr. Passaro:

You are a very well qualified candidate, and you did catch our eye during your interview, unfortunately, we are not going to offer you a position in our company at this time.

We wish you the best of luck in your life.

Respectfully,
Prudential Securities

Disappointment runs through my veins as quickly as it did when I first received this rejection notice back in 1992.

I remember being so mad at life at the time.

I just could not understand why this company did not hire me.

I remember taking the rejection hard.

I took it personally.

I remember, at the time, endlessly complaining nothing was going my way in life, and I deserved a break in life.

I deserved that job.

I was more than qualified.

I would have been very good at it.

Those were all true statements.

At the time, I was just too close to the puzzle to see the full picture.

I have since learned that life's pictures take time to fully develop.

I don't know what made me save this particular rejection notice, as I have had many others in my life I did not save.
But I did.

I haven't seen it in twenty-two years.

I don't know what made me look closer at the letter.

But I did.

My eyes froze on the return address of the letter.

One World Trade Center
55th floor.

With my outdated iPhone, I immediately Google my suspicion.

Yes, the 55th floor was exactly where the first plane hit the World Trade Center on 9/11.

I have often read stories of individuals, who were late to work on that dreadful day because they overslept, or their tire inconveniently went flat, or something told them to stay home on that fateful day.

I just never realized fate also detoured me from that building on that dreaded day.

It took me twenty-two years to understand why I didn't get that job.

Had I been hired, I might have been working on the 55th floor on that horrible day.
It makes one think.

You never know why things happen in life.

Sometimes the full picture of your life takes many years to develop.

I believe that everything in life is a co-orchestrated event; we just don't know or understand it at the time.

I believed that before my life's memories fell all over the floor.

I believe that even more now.
I think back to September 11th.

I was extremely fortunate on that dreaded day.

Evil plowed into so many lives on a day the sky was so blue.

I vividly remember the beauty of the sky on that day.

I also remember asking myself a few minutes later: "Why does God let bad things happen?"

I remember the day after our nations most horrific tragedy that we, as Americans, united.

Never before had the words:

United under God, indivisible, with Liberty and Justice for All.

Ever had more meaning to me.

On September 12th, the day after the most horrific experience the people of our nation have ever experienced, 238 million Americans were indoctrinated into "The Life-Changing Events Club."

A club you do not choose to join; one, which chooses you. A club no one ever wants to be part of, but once you are a member, you never want to give up your membership.

A club that transforms pain and hurt into life clarity and purpose.

A club that draws out of its members the greatest of the human spirit.

If you remember back to the two weeks after 9/11, starting on September 12th, you will recall the greatest two weeks of human spirit ever displayed in our countries history.

I vividly remember every car, driving on the road, having an American flag attached to its driver's side window, rapidly and proudly blowing in the wind.

No other time in my life was I ever more proud to be an American than in those two weeks that started on September 12th.
In America, on September 12th, there were no democrats or republicans, only leaders working together for the betterment of our country.

There were no strangers, only friends you hadn't met yet.

There were no blacks or whites, only fellow human beings needing comfort.

There was no hesitation to comfort someone who was in need.

We, as Americans, took action.
We reached out to people who needed our help.

Without being asked.

When we saw a person in need, we made that person feel loved, as best as we could.

We learned that words could never fully express our feelings, but our presence could.

Every person alive touched our soul.

Every life was important, every family was honored, and every breath was gold.

We united.
We helped.
We comforted.

And we consoled each other.

We were there for one another.

We treated each other with love.

I would never want to see any person of any generation, of any nation to ever experience anything like that dreaded day, ever again.

The combined pain and loss of our nation from that day is still incomprehensible and always will be.

It is amazing how it took adversity to bring the best out of all of us Americans.
We, as a country, as a human race, need to live every day like we did on September 12th.

"Dear Mr. Passaro:

You are a very well qualified candidate, and you did catch our eye during your interview, unfortunately, we are not going to offer you a position in our company at this time."

You never know why things happen in your life, but if you take notice, the answers will be revealed to you over time.

- 10 -
LISTEN, TRUST, ACT

Life is a succession of lessons
That must be lived
To be understood.

Helen Keller

I pick up off of the floor the original artwork for the logo of the Long Island Playmakers, a travel baseball team I founded in 2001.

The artwork is a silhouette of Derek Jeter, making an off-balance throw while suspended in mid-air.

My mind drifts back to the time when I *just knew* I had to form this team.

I have learned when there is a feeling brewing inside of you, tingling at your soul, you must listen to it without question.

Trust it without confirmation.

And act on it without hesitation or delay.

Disregard all logic, ignore the probabilities, and mute your ears to the naysayers.

The tingling is inside of you for a very distinct reason.

A reason that is so unique to you, to your life, and to your future happiness.

A reason, so profound, it cannot be comprehended in the present time, but its vast magnificence will one day reveal itself to you in splendor, at the absolute perfect moment in time.

That feeling brewing in your soul is absolutely on time and is precisely on point.

You need to believe that.

There is nothing more significant to your future happiness than for you to be in harmony with the magical feeling in your soul.

Listen to it, trust it and act on it.

Your reason, when revealed, will fill the synapsis between the how's and the why's of your life.

They say the soul is like a parent to us, guiding us and giving us great advice along our life's journey, and we are the child doing everything we can to ignore this advice.

Eventually, every child in the end finally understands their parent's advice was dead on, they just couldn't see or understand it at the time. Their life just needed time to develop.

One day in the future, when you are able to view your life looking backward, that inner feeling - your soul's advice to you - will unmask itself, and the pieces of your life's puzzle will come together.

Until then, while you are forced to view your life looking forward, that feeling may seem fragmented and insufficient.

Trust the gaps in rationale and in logic.

Make the leap of faith.

Your soul tingles for a reason.

That tingling is your soul's GPS system.

It knows.

It is able to see around corners, over mountains, and through the fog.

It will lead you to where you are meant to be at the exact moment you are meant to be there.

Listen to it.

Trust it.

Act on it.

And eventually, you will understand why the tingling was gnawing at your soul.

I know.

For I listened to mine.

In September of 2001, my soul tingled at the thought of building a youth baseball team to travel up and down the East Coast of the United States to compete in youth national baseball tournaments.

With nine-year-olds…

Believe me, as I am writing this I am snickering too.

At the time, my soul tingled at the thought of coaching and teaching young athletes life lessons through the sport of baseball.

The tingling told me to make it a top priority in my life.

Above all else.

It sounds absolutely crazy, I know...

My soul tingled at the thought of planning, training and coaching young athletes to compete at their highest level, on a national stage.

My soul tingled more intensely when I thought about teaching them how to win.

My soul led me to teach nine-year-olds about life through baseball.

I tried my best to dismiss the tingling feeling as being illogical and irrational.

It just didn't make sense.
Of course, it didn't make sense to me - I didn't have all the data at the time.

But my soul did.
What sane person builds a travel baseball team of nine-year-olds to travel up and down the East Coast of the United States?

"Why can't you just play in your neighborhood league?"

"Why is it so important for you to travel?"

I didn't have the answers to these obvious questions.

I just knew playing in our local youth baseball league was not what my feeling was telling me to do.

That just didn't make me tingle.

That is the only way I knew how to explain it.

No one understood it.

Including myself.

Never in my life had I ever experienced this type of inner knowing.

At first, I thought I was having a mid-life crisis.

I wasn't.

I had a great life, a great wife, and four healthy kids.

I loved everything about my life.

But the overwhelming tingling feeling just wouldn't go away.

"Why now?" I asked myself, trying to understand something that could not be understood at the time.

"There will be plenty of time to do this when the boys are older," I tried to rationalize to myself.

"Why now, why such a sense of urgency?"

My answer to those two questions was always the same:
"It makes me tingle."

I tried to pass the feeling off as being an irrational, fleeting thought that would eventually go away.

It did not.

Instead, the feeling intensified.

It demanded my attention.

It demanded that I listen to it.

It demanded that I trust it.

It demanded that I act on it.

Whenever the thought of building and coaching a youth baseball national tournament team entered my mind, it was as if I tapped into a vein of pure happiness.

Utopia.
I knew, I mean I just *knew*, I had to trust this feeling.

It was such a deep, never felt before kind of *knowing*, one I could not ignore.

So I didn't.

In 2001, despite the ridicule and against all logic, I succumbed and trusted my internal compass.
I just knew I had to.

Going against every logical and rational fiber in my body, I formed the Long Island Playmakers National Tournament Teams to travel up and down the East Coast of the United States.

I founded two teams in all, one for each of my sons.

And I made them my top priority in life.

Above all else.

I prioritized the teams above my work; above all of my non-baseball friends, and I even prioritized them above my extended family.

I am not saying this was right; I am just saying it was what I did.

Something was telling me it was that important.

I understood what I was doing was totally illogical and irrational, but I did it anyway.
The thing is, your soul doesn't live in a logical or rational world.

It is your soul; it lives in a spiritual, all-knowing world.

It lives in the purified air; air that is comprised of truth, love, belief and knowing. Knowing about everything, about everyone, everywhere, forever.

I believe your inner feelings are there to lead you on that path.
The path on which you experience your own unique journey.

The journey that is called life.

I believe every experience we go through in life is preparing us for what is to come in our lives.

To teach us the life lessons we need to know so we can best be prepared to handle our ultimate test, somewhere in the future.

I believe that our lives are an accumulation of life lessons that can only be learned by personal experience, to be completely understood.

Reading about a life lesson, or someone lecturing you about one, pales in comparison to feeling and experiencing that life lesson first hand.

I truly believe that.

I believe that the best way to teach someone something is to make that person believe they are learning something else.
I believe the universe does that to us.

It takes us on goals and missions in our lives we believe are the most important things to us at the time.

It does this to teach us lessons that we need to experience and learn, so we can successfully execute them when our real mission in life finally arrives.

I believe that if you really listen, your soul will talk to you.

All that we have to do is trust it, and act on it.

Throughout my Long Island Playmaker journey, I devoted six years of my life to building, coaching and traveling with twenty young athletes and their families up and down the East Coast of the United States, competing in the most competitive youth baseball tournaments in the country.

We played against every great team, on every great field, and in every great tournament.

Over those six years, I invested an insane amount of time, money and energy into youth baseball teaching young athletes life lessons through sport.

It was the number one priority in my life.

It seems absurd, doesn't it?

My mission was not only to teach young athletes how to hit, how to throw and how to catch a baseball; it was larger than that.

It was to teach them how to set a seemingly unachievable, dynamic goal and how to achieve that goal through belief, teamwork and by overcoming adversity.

In essence, my mission was to teach young athletes how to win at life.

As a team.

Yes, I valued, and I taught winning.

"Playing a game and not caring about winning is like being alive and not caring about living."
I also taught the value of a loss.

"It has to hurt. When it hurts, it means you care."
"When you care enough, you will figure it out."

"You will learn more from your losses than you will from your wins."

I taught unity:

"We win as a team, we lose as a team."

I taught about taking responsibility and about not making excuses:

"No blame, never blame. Blame is a loser's game.

Either you are part of the problem, or you are part of the solution."

I taught how to be a great teammate:

"Pick up your teammate when you see him down."

"The most valuable player on the team is the one that makes his teammates better."

I taught to sacrifice for the betterment of the team:

"A teammate is not someone who wears the same jersey as you, a teammate is someone for whom you would sacrifice and they for you."

I taught about how to focus in on what is important, the end goal:

"The goal is to score runs — you do that by getting someone on base, moving him over, and then someone driving him in.

I taught how to be the best at something:

"You need to live, breath and sleep it, 24 hours a day, 365 days a year. It can't be part of your life, it has to be your life."

I taught about selflessly filling roles that needed filling:

"There is no batting order —depending on when you come to the plate will dictate whether your mission is to get on, to move a teammate over, or to drive him in. Every one of those parts is equally important, without someone getting on, there is no one to move over or to drive in."

I taught about belief:

"The most valuable player on the team is the player who, when the team is down by a few runs in the seventh inning, still believes we can win. You don't need talent to do that, you need belief."

At the time, I didn't know why I had such an overwhelming desire to build the Long Island Playmakers, or why we had to be so competitive, or why teaching young athletes how to win was so important to me, or why I was so obsessed with teaching life lessons through the sport of baseball.

I just knew it was.

I mean it *really* was.
It was like nothing in the world mattered more.

And for those six years of my life, nothing else did matter more.

In total, over the six years, I coached both Long Island Playmakers teams in over 1,000 baseball games (no exaggeration); we competed in over 80 tournaments, and in 12 national tournaments, from Long Island to Florida.

We played in The Cooperstown Dreams Park Tournament eight times, the AAU Nationals twice; we played in almost every "Ripken" and "Sports at the Beach Tournament."

It was the best time of all of our lives.

Ask anyone who was part of it.

There is a quote from the movie, 'Friday Night Lights,' that says it best:

"When you look back at this time, I dare you to beat it. I just dare you."

That time in our lives will never be beaten.

Every tournament the team attended was a mini-vacation for every member of the team and their families.

We would load up our trucks, throw a luggage rack on the roof, and travel anywhere we could find a team as crazy as we were.

We stayed at countless hotels, we surrounded ourselves with great friends, we spent an insane amount of money, and yes, we played baseball, too.

Virtually every weekend for six years, both of the teams I coached competed against the best competition we could find. Then we would travel back home for five days of practice, fine-tune our game to play our next opponent, in our next event, the following weekend.

We repeated the process over and over again, for a brief six years.

I can't express the fun, the joy and the quality time my family and I experienced during those years or the intense relationships we formed with the other parents along the way.

The travel, the family time, the mini vacations, the camaraderie just could never be topped.

We were living the life of a professional youth baseball player, with one exception; it was like what Shoeless Joe Jackson said in the movie "The Field of Dreams:"

"We would have played for nothing."

We actually loved the sport so much we paid to play the game.

And that didn't bother us at all.

Practice, travel, play in a tournament and repeat it all over again the next weekend – all year long, for six years.

We traveled so much my four-year-old daughter at the time, Cassidy, actually thought the "Hampton Inn" was her home.

All throughout this great journey, I heard people ask:

"Why are you doing this?"

"Why are you investing so much time and effort into youth baseball?
"Aren't there more important things you could be doing?"

"Why don't you wait until the boys are 15 – when it really matters?"
Those questions were all legitimate ones – just ones I could not answer with any logic.

"Because I just know I have to do this, and I have to do this now, while the boys are young," I would answer outwardly.

Inwardly I said to myself, *"I'm doing all of this now because it makes me tingle."*
It really was baseball heaven.

Until it wasn't.

Like with all great things, the magical ride of the Long Island Playmakers eventually came to an end.

With success and high school approaching, the team transitioned from a team into a compilation of individuals, each with a different goal and agenda, not what I intended when I founded the organization.

It is exactly what happens when a member of a successful band wants to branch out on a solo career. It is impossible to be a member of a successful band and have a solo career at the same time; one will most definitely suffer.

One day, during the seventh year of the organization, I woke up to a coup where 90% of the players I had recruited, trained and coached for almost half of their life followed my assistant coach and started a new organization.

Absolute and total destruction.

One would think.
I did not.

My assistant coach took all of the Long Island Playmakers players, but he didn't take the most important part of the formula – my belief.

Instead of feeling sorry for myself or sitting there wallowing in the destruction of what had just happened, I decided to just build it again.

"There is no way you can recover – all the best players on the Island just left, who else is there to recruit?"

"You might as well just face the facts, it's over."

"It was a nice ride – just enjoy that it happened."

I heard over and over again by the baseball community.

I ignored the noise, and I listened to my soul.

My soul said to let it go, to not harbor any ill feelings about what had happened; that every ounce of my energies would be needed to build it again.

In my soul, I believed I could build it again.
I needed to do it all again.

So I did.

There were just six months to the start of the next season.

All "the best" players were unavailable.
The question of *"Why did they leave?"* hung over me.

None of that mattered to me.
I had total, illogical and irrational belief that I could and would build it again.

Something was telling me it was important to do so.

So I did.

The first thing I remember doing was eliminating the doubt; ignoring the odds and the difficulty of accomplishing this feat.

I just put my head down and went to work.

I believed and thus put myself in a position for good things to happen.

And over time they did.

Miraculously, there was a local team that had lost half of its team to a similar event.

We combined forces.

In just six short months, I had rebuilt a team that was ready for a competitive season.

The season arrived.

My new team made it to the finals in the very first tournament in which they ever played in.

And wouldn't you know it, our opponent in the championship game was my former team.

You can't make this stuff up.

I always said I could beat myself with someone else's team, and on that day I proved that arrogant phrase true.

That win, in that tournament, after having to start completely over after total destruction, taught me one of the greatest life lessons I have ever learned:

Behind love, belief is the second most powerful force on this earth.
When belief, love, and passion are combined, they produce growth.

Belief is not rational or logical.

It is magical.

People have always asked me if I hold a grudge against the assistant coach that poached my players and my team, and my answer is,

"I am so thankful he did, he taught me so much about belief.
I am sure it happened for a reason."

It absolutely did, and I would soon learn why.

A year after my Long Island Playmaker journey came to an end, life revealed to me the answers to all of those questions that had been asked of me during my baseball coaching years – all of the why's…

Why was it so important to me to train young athletes to compete at such a high level?

Why did we have to travel?
Why was I so obsessed with teaching life lessons through the sport of baseball?

What was the sense of urgency to do this while the boys were young instead of the more logical time when they were in high school?

Why did I need to prove that I was able to start over from absolute destruction?

On a normal day in August 2009, my son Maverick decided he no longer wanted to play the game of baseball – something deep down was telling him he shouldn't go to his game on that night.

Very contrary to my nature, I let him walk away.
Something inside of me said to let him do so.
It was on that night Maverick walked away from the game of baseball that all of those questions got answered.

It was on that night Jessica lost oxygen to her brain.

In just six minutes, my life changed forever.

Had Maverick gone to the game that night, we would not have been home to help Jess get medical attention.

The medical attention included putting Jess into a medically induced coma, to help her brain to heal.

My wife and I spent over 141 straight days with Jess in the hospital, at her bedside.

After the initial feeling of total destruction in my life, I knew the only way to rebound and rebuild was through my formula of:

Belief + Love + Passion = Growth.

I built a team of healthcare believers who believed in Jess's recovery.
The team worked in unison to achieve a dynamic goal – to have Jess recover to her maximum capacity.

When the doctors and hospitals felt they did all they could do for Jess, BettyJane and I took Jess home where we elected to be Jessica's *24 hours a day, 365 days a year* caregivers.

By choice.
"Sacrifice is giving up something you value, to get back something you value more in return."

Either I or BettyJane are with Jess at every moment of every day.

During the day, my wife takes care of Jess, and at nighttime, I do.

My wife and I have been outside of our house together only a few times over the last five years.

One of us is always at home with Jess.

Traveling together is not possible or plausible at this point in our lives.

That is our choice, one we would make over and over again.

There is nothing more important to us than to care for and cure our daughter.

While looking back at my life and trying to understand the how's and the whys of it all, it dawned on me why it was so important to build a team, to travel up and down the East Coast like there's no tomorrow, to teach young athletes life lessons through sport.

They say you teach best what you need to learn the most.

I believe that.
I suddenly realized my passion for teaching young athletes life lessons weren't for them.
It was for me.

I was being prepared by the universe for things I had no idea I needed preparing for.

It was so I could learn everything I needed to learn to be prepared when I face my real opponent, which was to become Jessica's caregiver.

Teamwork, belief, being a great teammate, sacrifice, yearning to win, overcoming total destruction, learning and rebounding from a loss, it all made sense now.

The best way to teach somebody something is to make them think they are learning something else.

I believe we go through certain experiences in our lives so we can learn the life lesson we will need to master - to beat a bigger, future opponent we will one day face.

I also believe these experiences have to be so important to us that we need to believe at the time, that it is all about them, but it is not.

They are just steps on the staircase to a higher, more important experience we will one day need to conquer.

That tingling inside of me was able to see years into the future and led me on a path that would best prepare me for what was to come.

I truly believe that.

Today, BettyJane and I are teammates.

Our family is our team.

It is the most important team I will ever be on.

Our goal is to score more runs than we give up, to be more happy than sad, to win the day, to win the game of life.

Our goal, just like everyone else's in this world, is to find happiness and meaning in our lives, to make a difference in our world, to matter.

We do that through caring for and curing Jess and by living and loving life.

We pick each other up constantly when the other one is down. It truly hurts because we care.

Over the six years, I learned how to build a team, to focus its players on one dynamic, seemingly unreachable goal.

"To have one head, ten hearts, and one beat."

The sacrifice for the betterment of our family BettyJane and I make every day was taught to me through the sport of baseball.

I can remember hearing myself say:

"Sacrifice is giving up something you value to have the possibility of getting something you value more in return.
No player wants to give up his at-bat and bunt, but he does it for the betterment of the team.
So the team can score a run.
And runs are what win ball games."

The same is in life.

As parents we make sacrifices. We give up things of value, so our families have the possibility of getting something greater in return.

"Take a pitch. It allows the base runner to steal a base and it wears the other pitcher down faster, and when he is tired, we will strike."

Nobody wants to give up what they value the most – their time and energy, but we do it so our families can win. As parents, we selflessly fill the role that is most needed by the team, our family. The role that is most needed in my family is the sacrificial role of being a caregiver. It is not glorious, or even pleasant, but it is what scores runs in our lives which helps my family to win each day.

"On this team, the guy who just gave up his at-bat and advanced a runner by a sacrifice bunt is met at the dugout steps with a high-five, just as if he had just hit a home run, that deserves our praise, that is what is going to make us win."

Being a caregiver is making the ultimate sacrifice in life. It is willingly exchanging time in your life to take care of a teammate.

"You are not a teammate because you wear the same jersey, you are a teammate because you would sacrifice for that person and they for you."

BettyJane and I willingly do this every day and will continue to do so indefinitely.

During my baseball coaching years, I taught the value of being a great teammate:

"Pick your teammate up when he is down."

The most important person on our family's team is the one who believes we can still win when we are down in the score, late in the game. There is nobody more important during a crisis than the individual who lifts his family's spirits, someone who makes everyone around him have belief and hope.

"The most valuable player on the team is not the player with the most talent, it is the player who makes his teammates better."

Over the six years I taught the importance of yearning to win:

"Yearning to win, catapults one to prepare to win, and that is what makes champions."

The desire to win in life is extremely important.

"Playing a ball game just to play the game and not to win the game is like being alive and not living."

When you care you find a way. You figure it out.

"It has to hurt if it hurts that is good - it means you care."

I taught to believe before most anyone in the world did.

"They could take away everything, and I can rebuild - as long as I have belief."

The ability to come back from seemingly absolute total destruction is possible as long as you believe when most wouldn't.

Currently, Jessica has made tremendous advancements on a relative scale.

A scale that started out with the starting line that was as close to death as one could be.

Today, Jessica is currently non-verbal and non-mobile, equidistant between death and life.

Which way that she will go will be based on love and belief.
It will be based on our ability to continuously have a big goal, to feel the reward is worth the effort.

I truly believe that.

It has taken an extreme amount of effort to get to this point.

We hold out hope and work towards the day when she improves as much as is possible for her to improve.

I truly don't feel like I am missing out on anything in life – taking care of my daughter is exactly where I want to be.

There are whole weekends where I do not leave a room now, or weeks that I do not leave the house, that is fine - as I have done enough traveling in my lifetime.

I write this story for a few reasons.

To let you know about the magnificence of your inner voice.

Without speaking, it will talk to you.

Listen to it, trust it, and act on it.

No matter how illogical or irrational its message may be.
It is always on time and exactly on point.

There is nothing more important to the overall joy and happiness of your life than to listen to your inner voice.
It is your soul, and your soul knows.

When you get a tingling inside of you, follow it.

It knows things you can't know right now.

Trust it more than anything in the world.
Act on it.
Eventually, you will understand why.

I write this story to relate to you the power of belief.

Believe in belief.

It is the second most important emotion in the world.

Dare to believe before anyone else does.

I write this story to relate to you the importance of teaching the yearning to win.

"Yearning to win catapults you into action, to prepare to win, it makes you expect great results and inspect your losses, to learn from them.

You will learn more from your losses than your wins."

I know I have.

Why does God let bad things happen?

I don't know the answer to that question yet, but I get the feeling that over time my life's picture will fully develop and the answer will be revealed to me, along with the trees grown from the seed of the greater good.

I look forward to being able to review the next twenty-two years of my life in retrospect.
I believe everything in life happens to you for a reason.
Every person you meet, you meet for a reason, at the right time, at precisely the right moment, and then they move on.

When you have the opportunity to look back at your life all of the pieces do come together.

All of the experiences do combine to create a total picture.

Are all of the things that will happen in life fair or just?

Most definitely not, but magically that too is part of the universes formula.

How?
Only the universe knows at the time.

We eventually find out.

Until then keep living.

Keep feeling.

Keep loving.

Keep moving forward.

The universe is more complex than we can ever imagine.
Eight billion pieces are being juggled by the universe all at once, all intertwined, all interconnected.

The universe is complex, but it is very simple.

It runs on love.

'More love' solves everything.

So keep putting your pieces together.

Keep loving.

Keep believing.

Keep living forward so when the right time comes, you can review your life in reverse and understand.

I put the artwork of the Long Island Playmakers logo and all the other pieces to the puzzle of JohnA Passaro back into my box, and I put the box back on the top shelf.

I take a deep breath as I have a renewed faith that everything in life happens the way it is supposed to happen.

Or else it would have happened differently.

- 11 -
MORE LOVE

The one thing that you can't take away from me
Is the way that I choose to respond
To what you do to me.
The Last of one's freedom
Is to choose one's attitude
In any given circumstance

Victor Frankl
A Mans Search for Meaning.

November 2014

It has been six weeks since I originally stood in line at the AT&T store.

My iPhone 6 Plus has finally arrived.

I open the box to the phone with great enthusiasm; I just can't wait to use this new device.

Before I actually use the iPhone, I go to the settings section, and I adjust every default pre-set by Apple.

The default setting is probably what the masses would want, but not what I want.

After many adjustments, I am now ready to use my iPhone.

The adjustments I have made will allow me to have the most personable, enjoyable experience possible.

As I use my iPhone for the first time, a thought comes to my mind.

I find it to be very ironic that I wouldn't use my new iPhone without changing the factory default settings but I have lived most of my life without changing the emotional default settings I was born with.

One of the keys in life is to know enough to reset your emotional default settings to not have the normal reaction to things.

Your brain is as vast as a supreme being. To tap into your brains unlimited powers, you need to reprogram your thinking.

No one ever teaches you this, but once learned this will catapult you into your ultimate level of happiness, it is sort of like acquiring a cheat code for a video game, it will take you to places most others will never see, except it is not cheating, it is a gift.

It is time to adjust all of my emotional default settings in my life to "More Love."

When family or friends disappoint me by acting out in a way that is not them, instead of showing my disappointment, I will act with "More Love."

When a senseless world event destroys human life, I will change my default settings from "Callousness" to "More Love."

When a problem exists that I do not currently have a viable solution for I will change my default setting from Fear to "More Love."

When the future does not look attractive enough to want to enter into, I will change my default setting from Despair to "More Love."

When someone harms me without any regard to my being, I will change my default setting from Hatred to "More Love."

When someone else finds success at what I have been working hard to achieve, I will change my default settings from Jealousy to "More Love."

When someone wrongs me, I will change my default setting from holding a grudge to "More Love."

Not forgiving someone to "More Love."

Now I am ready to have the most enjoyable experience possible from my life.

- 12 -

I Hear You

When the scientists of the future
Show up at my house with robot eyes
And they tell me to try them on,
I will tell the scientists to screw off,
Because I do not want to see
A world without Augustus Waters.

Isaac
(Augusts's friend who is blind)
The Fault In The Stars

December 2014

I am sitting on my couch watching a television show called "The Voice," the show where four rock stars sit in Star Trek looking chairs with their backs turned to the performer. It is the performer's job to get at least one of them to turn around with just the sound of their voice.

Cassidy is sitting next to me, and Jess is across the room in her bed.

Out of the corner of my eye, I notice Cassidy is visibly upset.

"Cassidy, why do you look so sad?"
"Do you really want to know?"
"Yes, I do."

"I can't remember Jess's voice anymore."

She breaks my heart a little more when she says: "I just want to be able to talk with my older sister."

I'm caught off guard.

I should have realized that Cassidy just recently became a teenager and is dealing with an assortment of new and different emotions.

I say, "Cassidy, voices may fade but love never will."

She looks at me, wipes the tears from her eyes, forces a smile and says, "But I would love to hear her voice just one more time."

"I hear you, Cassidy, I hear you."

- 13 -

THE JUNGLE

All the world's a stage,
And all the men and women merely players;
They have their exits and their entrances;
And one man in his time plays many parts.

William Shakespeare

There is a scene in the movie "Forrest Gump" where Forrest is fighting for his life, running to safety out of the Vietnam jungle. He is on a clear path that would get him out of the jungle and away from the enemy when he suddenly realizes some soldiers from his platoon are still in the jungle, still in danger, and are unable to find their own way out.

Upon realizing this, Forrest reverses his course and heads back into the jungle, into danger, to help bring the soldiers from his platoon back to safety.

Under enemy attack, one by one, Forrest carries the soldiers out of the jungle to the shore, to relative safety.

All during this process, Forrest ignores his own peril as he strives not to leave anyone behind.

I, like Forrest, decided to re-enter the jungle every day.
There are days when I have a clear path to get out of the jungle, and I mentally decide to reverse course and re-enter the jungle to bring my platoon, my family, out toward safety.

This happens quite often as BettyJane ignores her own peril and is reluctant to seek safety knowing one of her own is still in danger.

BettyJane is Lieutenant Dan, as she feels it is more honorable for one to go down with their men in battle rather than move on without them.

There are days where I literally have to pick her up off of the ground, fallen from exhaustion and carry her to the shore.

She refuses to voluntarily cross that line, as she sees moving forward as a betrayal of sorts.

Like Lieutenant Dan, she feels it is her duty to never leave the jungle until every one of her troops is accounted for.

Even if it means, giving up her life in the process.

There are days when she fights with me as I attempt to carry her back onto safe ground.
Just as Lieutenant Dan punched and kicked Forrest when he picked him up and carried him to the shore just before a sure fatal air attack destroyed his previous location.

BettyJane can't see being happy until she knows her platoon is all accounted for.

Day after day, with safety available, she stays in the jungle.

She wants to hurt.

"When you hurt, you figure it out," she says to me.
"I need to figure this out, I have to hurt."

- 14 -
MR. DUPLICITY

The greatest hazard of all,
Losing one's self,
Can happen very quietly in the world,
As if it were nothing at all.
No other loss can occur so quietly.
Any other loss – an arm, a leg, five dollars, a wife
Is sure to be noticed.

Soren Kierkegaard
The Sickness unto Death

January 2015

I don't know when it occurred; I just know one day it did without my ever noticing.

I do not cry every day anymore.

Come to think of it, I actually can't remember the last time I had to turn away to hide my tears from the world.

That realization upsets me.
"If it hurts, it means you care.

If you care, then you will figure it out."

Being I haven't cried recently, does that mean I am starting to hurt less?

To care less?

Have I moved on?

Have I left Jess behind in the jungle?

I have to keep hurting.

I have to figure this out.

Rumi wrote: *"The cure for the pain is in the pain."*

I force myself to cry.

I force myself to cry a hard, deep cry.

I am in a quandary, I want to maximize my hurt, but yet I want to be able to keep moving forward.

I am very good at doing one thing at a time extremely well. It is my personality to focus to near obsession to get the results I want.

I am very bad at handling two things at one time.

My nature is to give 100% of myself to a goal; to have two goals at the same time would then require I would need to have 200%, which I do not have.
That is just how my mind works.

How do I move forward *and* stay behind at the same time?

I have a demolition derby of contradictory emotions taking place inside of me at all times.

If I move in two opposite directions with the same force, I will be sure to go nowhere.

Then it hits me.

If Forrest didn't clear his platoon from the jungle, they all would have surely died from that air strike.

I got to make sure everyone is out of the jungle.

I have to find a way to keep moving forward without feeling I am moving on.

- 15 -

THE FORMULA

The only guarantee
Is that you get a dash,
—
A date when you are born
And a date that you died,

Whether you live in between
Is up to you.

I am alone with Jess.

I am giving BettyJane some much-needed time out of the house to rejuvenate her mind and her body.

She is reluctantly visiting with her mom for the better part of the next two days.

It is at these times, when I watch Jess for days at a time, that my mind and life become still.

It is this stillness that allows me to tap into my inner voice.

I am watching Oprah's "Master Class" on TV, listening to Billy Bob Thornton talk about losing his brother:

"I have never been the same since my brother died.
There is a melancholy in me that never goes away.

I'm 50% happy and 50% sad at any given moment.

The only advice that I can give people when you lose someone like that is

"You won't ever get over it."

And the more you know that, and embrace it, the better off you are.

I don't want to forget my brother, and I don't want to forget what it felt like when he died because he deserves it - that's how important that he was to me.

So if I have to suffer and I have to be sad for the rest of my life, and I have to be lonely without him, then that's the way I will honor him."

As someone with a very competitive personality, I do not believe in ties.

I believe there always has to be a winner.

As a father, I do not believe I have lost Jess.

I believe it is a gift BettyJane and I have the opportunity to get Jess incrementally better each day, over time.

In my mind, I take Billy Bob Thornton's formula, and I adjust it ever so slightly.

I decide I will cap my melancholy at 49% at any given time to leave room for me to be 51% happy in my life.
Moving forward without leaving Jess behind.
When Jessica lost oxygen to her brain for six minutes, my grief and sadness were overwhelming.

I wanted to feel 100% sadness and grief.

Like Billy Bob Thornton said, I felt she deserved that.

That's how important she is to me.

There is an old wrestling adage that says:

"Don't let one loss defeat you twice."

And then I realized, if I felt 100% sadness all the time, then at least two people and probably more would be lost by this tragedy.

I could not let that happen.

Life is a gift.

It is a miracle.

To voluntarily not live it, and not enjoy it, is insane.

Thoreau gave the best advice and wrote me a personal prescription when he said:

"If you want to be happy, be."

So I decided to be.

Always.

Under all conditions.
50% happy and 50% sad at all times doesn't work for me.

Abraham Lincoln commented, "People are as happy as they decide to be."

I decided to always be more happy than sad.

51% happy, 49% melancholy, works for me.

That allows me to win the day.

Keep moving forward, without leaving Jess behind.

- 16 -

EARN YOUR WAY

All the adversity I've had in my life,
All my troubles and obstacles have strengthened me.
You may not realize it when it happens,
But a kick in the teeth
May be the best thing in the world for you.

Walt Disney

There is a time each day, before my eyelids open, when I almost forget my circumstances, my battle, my mission, it is a time when I do not have to fight to feel happy, I just am.

It lasts for a millisecond each day, but it exists.

And I hold onto that feeling all day.

The rest of my happiness I need to fight for, I need to earn.

Each day, upon my realization I am entering a new day to fight again, I mentally adjust my mind for another battle.

I know I have work to do, as I enter each new day automatically behind in the score:

Melancholy - 49%
Happiness – 0%
Each day that starts anew starts with me being 49% sad, crushed, an emotional wreck, in the abyss of emotional torture.

That's the given.

The good news is I still have room to earn 51% happiness, enough to win the day.

51% beats 49%.

So every day my job is to gain that 51%.

To win the day.

The late Stuart Scott said it best in his 2014 ESPY's speech when he said:

"You beat cancer by how you live, why you live, and in the manner in which you live."

I need to earn my 51% of happiness each day by how I live, why I live and in the manner in which I live:

By improving the quality of other people's lives, by finding goodness and meaning and by spreading kindness and love.

Every time I find goodness or meaning and spread kindness or love, I earn points for the day.

My goal is to earn 51 percentage points each and every day, to be more happy than sad.

To make the world a better place.

And when I am able to do that, then I am able to win the day. I have realized my being happier than sad does not diminish the significance of what has happened to Jess.

It actually honors her by my ability to make the world just slightly better each day.

It isn't easy.

I have no room for error.

Even 1% more on the negative side and I would lose the day.

And I hate losing.

I have no room to feel sorry for myself.

I have no room for any negative emotions.

I have no room for sarcasm.

No room for cynicism.
No room to be callous.

No room to be apathetic.

No room to be uncaring.

To make up the 51%, I need to earn each % point.

I need to capitalize on every opportunity that presents itself to gain on my deficit.

Compliments, compassion and action gain me positive points.

Love, caring, and empathy are even greater points.

I look for every opportunity to spread kindness, no matter how small.

I need every % point to overcome my daily deficit.

I can't end the day if there is 1% more I could do.

So I reach out to a friend in need.

I smile at a stranger walking by.

I reacquainted with a friend from high school.

I write a letter to someone whom I hadn't seen in decades.
I do something for someone has no chance of ever repaying me.

At the end of each day, I do not put my head on the pillow until I have tallied up the necessary 51% of happy points.

I find when I win the day my soul talks to me, and when I don't win the day my soul is silent.

A silent soul is a wasted soul, so each day my goal is just to hear my soul speak to me.

Spreading love and kindness puts my soul in a talking mood.

The more love and kindness I spread, the more my soul talks to me.

There is nothing more I desire than to hear my inner voice.

Each day I fan the flame of my soul by spreading love.

My goal is to make love from my heart go viral each day, so the sound of my soul goes viral in my inner mind.

I have learned the trick to kindness is time.

I have learned the reason people are callous or insensitive is that their lives are too full.

They don't have any more space in their lives.

Even for kindness.

I have learned the best thing one can do is to de-clutter their lives to always have space, hence time, to be kind.

The ability to take time to be kind to someone in this world is the ultimate entry into your soul.

It is one of life's greatest ironies that people are so busy in their life trying to be happy when all they have to do is slow down and have the time to be kind.

Leave some space in your life to have the time to be kind.

- 17 -
A STRETCH AND A SMILE

Will today be the day?
I don't know.
It is the possibility that keeps me going
And not the guarantee.

Noah Drake
The Notebook

In Nicholas Sparks "The Notebook," an older Noah Drake reads to his aging wife, Ally, trying so desperately to help her remember moments of their life together.

Ally is battling the advancing stages of Alzheimer's.

There is one scene in particular where Noah is approaching Ally's room in the nursing home, and right before he gets to her door he wonders to himself,

"Will today be the day?"

The day Ally will remember Noah, and their life together, for a few precious moments.

In her life, Jessie read approximately one hundred books.

Actually, she read the same book one hundred times.

That book was "The Notebook."

There wasn't a day that went by when Jess didn't read from The Notebook.

I would find it under her pillow as she slept each night.

And when Jess wasn't reading the book, she was watching the movie.

I remember one day asking her: "Jess, you haven't finished that book yet?"

And she responded: "I have, dad, but I just keep reading it over and over again. It just touches my soul."

Little did I know in a few short years life would audition me for the real-life role as Noah, and Jess for Ally.

"Will today be the day?"
Each of my days starts the same.

With hope.

Could today be the day that we get a breakthrough?
The day that Jess is able to verbally communicate with us.
I don't know why but in her sleep Jess becomes alive.

While Jess is sleeping her arms and legs, move uninhibited, but as soon as she awakens, her limbs contract again into non-mobility. Each day as she awakens from her sleep, there is a fifteen-second window that Jess is able to stretch on her own.

I mean a huge stretch.

A body twisting, head turning, moaning, groaning stretch.

This fifteen-second window each day is the closest that I get to "BJ," -Before Jess.

This is the time that Jess most resembles her former self.

It is for a very short time each day, and then it disappears quicker than a summer sun on the horizon.

When she first awakens, Jess's yawning and facial expressions are identical to when she was a healthy teenage girl attending college.

Each morning I get a glimpse of hope that lasts less than a quarter of a minute.

Those fifteen seconds of a miracle, fuel me for the rest of my day.

After Jess physically stretches on her own, her body goes into contraction, as she is unable to move her limbs for the rest of the day.

After this contraction is complete, I stretch Jess myself.

I start by pressing on Jess's feet - feet that are so rigid.

I press against that rigidity, and after a few seconds, I can suddenly feel life in Jess's feet pushing back.

I can feel life inside of Jess's feet attempting to break out.

It's the greatest feeling.

It is, for both of us, the best part of our days.

Mine, because I know Jess is there, and hers because she knows I am there for her, I haven't given up on her.
Moving forward without moving on.

I end the stretching of Jess's feet by touching her two big toes together.

Zihuatanejo.

And a flood of belief fills me as I remember the first time she did the same in the hospital after her injury.

That memory re-instills in me an inner knowing that Jess is present inside of her body. A body that has had an avalanche in her mind, an avalanche from which, each day, I attempt to clear a path for her to reemerge.

After I touch Jess's two big toes together, I then proceed to Jess's arms. I stretch them, without breaking them in two.

I start out by really pulling hard on her arms, pulling them out of their contracted position. It almost feels as if I am going to snap Jess's arms off her body, sort of like pulling too hard on one side of a turkey's wishbone.

After I get each arm out of its tight contraction, Jessie's arm muscles start to tremble, and then they release from their contraction and glide higher on their own as if a lock has been released.

They glide until her arms are stretched upwards as far as they can go, and then they retract back into paralysis.

And I must go to work.

- 18 -
WHAT I KNOW FOR SURE

I am nothing special;
Of this I am sure.
I am a common man with common thoughts,
And I've led a common life.
There are no monuments dedicated to me
And my name will soon be forgotten,
But I've loved another with all my heart and soul,
And to me,
This has always been enough.

Noah Drake
The Notebook

January 2015

Everyone alive at one time or another has fancied themselves becoming somebody, doing something with their life.

I am no exception.

Today I turn 50 years of age.

My initial reaction to turning 50 was I felt I hadn't done anything with my life; I hadn't become anyone.
Then I look across the room at Jess and I know one thing for sure.

I know my family knows I love them.

Unconditionally.

No matter what.

Through anything.

And that is who I am - who I have become.

And it is this knowledge which makes me feel I have achieved man's greatest accomplishment.

That my life has meaning, that I matter, that I have made a difference in my family's world and that I have somehow made the world a better place.

- 19 -
#119,104

Many of the things
That you can count,
Don't count.
Many of the things
That you can't count,
Really count.

Albert Einstein

#119,104

Understanding those six numbers are more valuable for experiencing happiness in one's life, than knowing the next six winning lotto numbers.

Those are the numbers the Nazis branded on the forearm of Victor Frankl when they held him prisoner in Auschwitz.

By suffering through the worst event humanity has ever seen, Victor Frankl was able to find the worlds greatest secret.

In his book, "Man's Search for Meaning," Frankl writes:

"I grasped the meaning of this greatest secret.

The salvation of man is through love and in love.

The truth is that love is the ultimate and the highest goal to which man can aspire.

That human life, under any circumstances, never ceases to have a meaning."

I guess I have achieved more than I had previously thought.

I have grasped the meaning of life's greatest secret.

- 20 -
RUNNY KNOWS

It is what it is.
Sometimes you don't see what it is
Until you see what it is.
Then, it is what it is.

I Bought a Zoo

February 2015

I know I should run.

But I don't.

I rationalize to myself that I can't.

I can't embarrass someone like that.

I am trapped between shopping carts in a checkout line at the supermarket.

All of my items I am purchasing on this day are on the conveyer belt, ready to be scanned and bagged by the cashier - the cashier who is using one hand to scan each item while her other hand is wiping her nose.
I know I should run from this runny nose clerk, but I am trapped, I can't go back, and I can't go forward.

Snot Lady is going to touch every one of the items I am purchasing today.

For most, seeing a cashier wipe her nose a few times would definitely give one the koodies, but for me, it gives me the chills; a six-month hospital stay for Jess flashes through my mind.

As my order approaches the cashier on the conveyor belt, the absolute worst possible thing happens.

The cashier switches hands.

The hand she was using to wipe her nose, she is now using to scan my groceries.

I am now playing Russian roulette having five bullets in the chamber, instead of just one.

I am always so careful, and I try to be as polite as I can, but my life is different. I detour from sneezes or coughs in a crowd, and I always run from runny noses.

I try not to be rude, but sometimes it is quite obvious I just up and leave at the first sign someone has a cold.

I have to; colds to Jess inevitably turn into pneumonia, which turns into a spin of the cylinder - playing Russian roulette with our lives.

I don't know what makes me stay online today.

Maybe it is wishful thinking, or maybe I realize this is the same cashier who was so nice to Cassidy last week when she asked her about her school soccer season.
But whatever it is that causes me to stay, I stay.

Even knowing it is a mistake.

A rookie mistake.
And I am not, by any means, a rookie at this.

I know I should run from this runny nose, but I do not.

"John, what are you doing? You can't spray Lysol on the groceries!" BettyJane screams at me as she walks into the kitchen as I am trying to decontaminate what I just purchased from the supermarket.

"BettyJane, I just made a rookie mistake. I allowed Snot Lady to check me out at the grocery store, I know I should have run, but I didn't. If I can't spray Lysol on all of this, then we need to throw it all away."

"John, you're NOT spraying Lysol on anything, and we are NOT throwing $400 worth of groceries away! Relax, you are probably exaggerating what you think you saw, Jess will be fine, she doesn't eat this food anyway."

"No, but we touch it when we eat it and then we will transfer it to her when we feed her."

Then BettyJane gave me a look, a look which said,

"We have been through so much, and we have never once fought with each other. And now we're going to fight about whether you should Lysol our food or not?"

I stop; I let it go; I know she's right.

But I know that I, too, am right.

I should have run.

I should have just left $400 of groceries on that conveyer belt, made some sort of excuse and got away from the Snot Lady.

Fear starts to rise up in my stomach.

- 21 -

SNORKELING

My head is under water,
But I am breathing fine.

John Legend
All of Me, Loves All of You.

On our honeymoon back in 1989, BettyJane and I decided to go snorkeling.

We took a boat ride for what seemed to be miles from the shore.

Along the way, we ate fresh fruit, shrimp and sipped champagne.

We were just absolutely enjoying life.

The water was picturesque, see-through, actually white with a tint of turquoise.

When we arrived at the snorkeling destination, we were given instructions on how to put our face in the water and still breathe with the snorkel tube just inches out of the water. We were given flippers to put on and were directed to where the most colorful fish could be found.
BettyJane has always had a unique comedic quality about her when she does something for the first time.
On that day she was struggling to put on her snorkeling equipment.

Every time she made an adjustment, she would inadvertently un-adjust another part of her equipment.

It was sort of like an Abbot and Costello episode.

Viewing this comedic skit was normal for me, so I just laughed and allowed BettyJane to adjust and readjust her mask on her own, knowing she would eventually get it right.

The tour instructors didn't know her like I did and gave BettyJane an undue amount of attention, which only made the adjusting process funnier to watch.

BettyJane was laughing her head off with each pull of the strap of her goggles and snorkel, one pull making the goggles too tight and the next making them too loose.

She soon realized I was patiently waiting for her, and she yelled out to me,

"Go ahead, I will only be a second. I will meet you out there."

As I was letting her know I would wait for her, the tour guide pulled too hard on one of her goggle straps, breaking it in two.

Everyone laughed.

As BettyJane leaned over to pick up her broken strap, she broke her acrylic nail, which fell into the water.
Instantaneously, all three instructors jumped overboard in search of her nail.

The nail floated to the bottom of the water.

Somehow, in crystal clear, see-through water, it could not be found.

BettyJane assured me she would meet me out in the water in a few minutes, so I started to wade out on my own.

With each step away from the boat the clear water inched up my chest.

The vastness of the water struck me.

Silence came alive.

The only two things I could hear were the sounds of water droplets reentering the water and BettyJane's conversation with the crew back at the boat.

"Why is this the spot where we stopped, I mean we were traveling for a while, and we stopped in *this* exact spot – why is that?"

BettyJane inquisitively asked the crewmembers.

And without any hesitation one of the crew members replied,

"We come here to get away from the sharks."

Now, I don't know if he was serious, half serious or just having some fun with a naïve tourist, but the thought of sharks got into my head.
Fixing BettyJane's broken strap took longer than expected, which gave me plenty of time to wade far away from the boat.

I could still see BettyJane on the boat, but with each step, they were getting pretty small on the horizon.

I remember the awesome beauty of the water, how crystal clear and gorgeous it was.

I walked a few more minutes just admiring the colorful fish from the view above the surface of the water.

I could no longer see the boat.

I had yet to put my face in the water and use my snorkel to breath air.

It was time.

I put my mask on; I blew the air out of the air tube, I put my goggles on and put my face into the water.

My head was underwater and I was breathing fine.

Fine, up until the thought of sharks reemerged.

Fear appeared and started to work its way up my chest.

What if…

What if the crew was wrong?

What if there were sharks here?

What if I put my head in the water too far and sucked in water and not air?

I never had a panic attack in my life.

Up until this point.

All of a sudden, every one of my thoughts was engulfed with fear; each played out the worst-case scenario and then, quickly magnified it.

Within two minutes, my mind was consumed with the thought if I went down now, no one would ever know what had happened to me, or would ever find me.

I was wading in water in which I could stand, but I was afraid of drowning.

My mind had created a scenario that elicited extreme fear and panic, and that is exactly how my body reacted.

I was able to breathe, but I feared that I was going to drown.

All because of a shark, that wasn't there.

It was at that time I remembered BettyJane on the boat, laughing at every adjustment that either made her mask so tight, it cut off her circulation, or so loose, the mask dangled loosely around her neck.

In an instant, my mind shifted its focus from fear to love.

My body relaxed, my mind slowed, and the fear went away.

I started walking back towards the boat.

The sight of the boat became bigger and bigger with each passing second.

The water started to subside from my chest; moving lower down my waist with each advancing step.

I made it all the way back to the boat by redirecting my fear back towards my love.
Victor Frankl wrote,

"I understood how a man who has nothing left in this world still may know bliss, be it only for a brief moment, in the contemplation of his beloved."

Famous boxing trainer Cus D'Amato once told a young Mike Tyson,

"Fire can either heat your house, or it can burn it down, it is all whether you control it, or it controls you."

Fear is fire.

And the antidote to fear is love.

- 22 -
AVERTING A CRASH

Your soul will speak to you
In whispers,
And when you don't pay close enough attention,
It will roar.

I am driving on the Long Island Expressway, heading home.

I am in no hurry, and there is no traffic.

I am in the right-hand lane.

I am neither tail gaiting, nor am I speeding.

A feeling comes over me that I should get into the far left-hand lane.

For no reason.

So I do.

As soon as I get over to the left-hand lane, the car ahead of me in the right-hand lane, from where I have just come, has a blowout.

His tire explodes.

His car uncontrollably does a one-eighty and is now facing oncoming cars.

I would have been the first oncoming car, had I not switched lanes.

The man that just had the blowout is able to miraculously maneuver to the shoulder of the highway, averting all danger.

I watch all of this from my rear view mirror as I continue home safely.

Halfway home I realize this has been the third such occurrence that has happened to me in the last two weeks. The other two occurrences were similar, not as extreme, but eerily similar.

Having a feeling to switch lanes, and averting danger by listening to and acting on that feeling.

I wrote the other two times off as just being lucky; this one has changed my mind.

With this latest occurrence, I now believe the Universe is communicating with me, trying to get my attention, so I listen to the feeling in my soul.

I believe there is something important the Universe is going to be telling me soon, and it wants my utmost attention.

Which it now has.

I am now paying close attention, and trusting my inner voice, as I believe it is about to save me from crashing for a fourth time.

- 23 -
THE FIGHT OF YOUR LIFE

There are victories
Of the soul and spirit.
Sometimes,
Even if you lose,
You win.

Elie Wiesel

When I was growing up, my father worked the lobster shift, from 4-12 midnight.

He took the train from Long Island to New York City each day.

To have use of the car for the night, I would drive my father to the train station every day.

On April 15th, 1985 we were on our way to the train station, and I was just about to make the turn into the station when my father said to me, "John, keep going."

"What do you mean, keep going?" I asked him.
"Just keep driving until I tell you to stop."
Not knowing what his reasoning was, I obliged.
After a few minutes, I asked him, "Dad, where are we going?"

"We're going to the fight."

My heart started pounding, and my foot stepped on the gas pedal just a little harder.

"The fight," was Hagler vs. Hearns.

In retrospect, it turned out to be the greatest fight in the history of boxing.

I remember sitting in the arena with my dad, watching the pay per view of the fight.

My responsible father, the one who followed his intuition to play hooky from work to take his kid to go watch a fight, and was rewarded by the universe to be able to witness the greatest fight of the century.

I remember the first round action between Hagler and Hearns.

The action was non-stop; the pace was relentless.

Both fighters went toe to toe for the full three minutes.

I remember thinking there was no way they could possibly keep up that pace.

And they didn't.

Hagler knocked out Hearns in three rounds.

Those three rounds are thought to be the most action-packed, greatest three rounds in the history of the sport.
After the fight, my father turned to me and said,

"John, there is going to be a time in your life when you are going to be in the fight of your life, and that's how I want you to fight."

"Like Hagler?" I asked.

"Like either one of those fighters, they both gave everything they had, there were no losers in that fight tonight."

- 24 -

A DARK NIGHT OF THE SOUL

In the middle of the journey of my life,
I found myself in a dark wood,
For I had lost the right path.
Eventually,
I would find the right path,
But in the most unlikely place.

Dante

In the movie "The Million Dollar Baby," female boxer Mattie Hayes, through her persistence, hard work, and proper training, gets a million dollar championship fight.

In that fight she gets sucker punched, loses her balance and on the way down to the canvas, she hits her head on the stool in her corner and breaks her neck, thus making her a quadriplegic for life.

After months in the hospital on a ventilator, she begs Frankie, her trainer, for a favor.

She asks him to turn her breathing machine off.

"I can't be like this Frankie, not after what I have done.
I've seen the world.

People have chanted my name, well not my name, but some damn Gaelic nickname that you gave me "Mo Cuishle."
I was born two pounds six ounces.

My daddy always used to tell me that I had to fight to get into this world, and I'd fight on my way out.

That's all that I want to do, Frankie. I just don't want to fight you to do it."

After an internal battle, Frankie kisses Maggie on her forehead, and then reluctantly shuts off Maggie's breathing machine.

He whispers under his breath, "Mo Cushlie," which means

"My darling, my blood."

Even though Frankie didn't believe in what Maggie asked him to do, he loved her enough to want to end her suffering.

He did it to stop an unfair, mismatched fight, one in which she could no longer defend herself.

He did it even though it went against every fiber of his being.

Any good corner man knows when to throw in the towel.

He knows when his boxer has had enough, when they are defenseless when they are taking an unrelenting pounding.

A good corner man realizes when the fight needs to come to an end.
They know when they just can't be witness to the beating anymore.

When enough, is enough.

So the corner man takes the towel that he has been holding onto for the last few rounds, he hesitates for one more second hoping for a miracle, when that miracle never arrives he raises his arm and throws the towel into the center of the ring.

And just like that - the suffering stops.

It is a rather hard night of caregiving.

I knew I should have run when I saw the grocery clerk wipe her nose.

As I feared, Jess has gotten sick just a few short days after I went grocery shopping and allowed Snot Lady to check me out.

Jess is so congested. Her nose is totally clogged, and she just can't adjust to breathing out of her mouth on her own.
It is pure hell to see her battle for every breath.

It is an even hotter hell knowing her suffering is due to my decision to stay on Snot Lady's line at the grocery store.

This night never seems to end.

I have spent the last few hours listening to Jess gasp for air.

Every breath is a battle.
She battles for air 60x a minute, 3,600x an hour and 14,400x over the course of half of the night.

It is soul crushing to listen to.

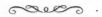

It is deep into the night, and I am floating somewhere between light sleep and consciousness.

Resting, yet on red alert.

It is the place where my subconscious takes over my conscious.

Imagine driving home from a long journey, late at night and pulling into your driveway, opening your eyes and having no idea how you got home safely.

But you did.

That's the place where I reside every night.

Except with being a caregiver, the only difference is you are behind the wheel, your eyes are open, you see things, horrible things, and you have no control of the steering wheel.

Sometimes you end up back in your driveway, and sometimes you end up in a ditch screaming for help in the middle of nowhere, and no one can hear you.
Both events are equally scary.

Although the time you end up in the ditch is more valuable, you have to find your own way back home.

And that ride you will remember.
Forever.

This place where you have no control where you land and have to find your own way home, I have come to learn is known as the dark night of my soul.

It is an event which is designed to bring you to the abyss and back, but only if you want to come back; only if you can find your way back.

Lessing once said, *"There are things which must cause you to lose your reason, or you have none to lose."*
I am currently having a dream about my father, the only dream I have ever have had of him since his passing.

In my dream, he is walking out of the forest, with his legs intact and his jeans on, with a full head of hair; not the seventy-year-old thin hair version of him but a combination of a forty-something and a mature man version.

He looks like he was just released from a long journey through many forests.

He looks weathered, but grateful like he found out a secret, one he promised he would never tell.

He is holding one acorn between his thumb and forefinger.

He is taking short steps without bending his knees, walking like someone who just experienced a traumatic event, but has endured it and knows now that he is safe.

I don't know why but my initial reaction to seeing him walk out of the forest is to try to take a selfie with him. I approach him, I put my arm around him, and we pose for a picture.

The flash goes off, but when I look down at my iPhone, he is not in the picture.

It is just the acorn and me.

That bothers me, deeply.

He then turns to me and says,

"Do what you want to do John.

Trust yourself."

And just like that, he disappears.

The acorn is left behind.

I faintly hear a gurgling sound like someone is drowning.

I hear it, but I do not know where it is coming.
Is it reality?

Is it my dream?

I suddenly realize the gurgling sound is real and is coming from Jess who is sleeping just a few feet from me.

During the night I constantly have to adjust Jess's head position as she sleeps; if it is too far back she chokes, and if it is too far forward her head falls face first into a pillow.

While I attempt to sleep, I am awakened by the faint muffled sound of Jess struggling for air.
Based on the gurgling sound I realize Jess's head is too far back and she is choking on her saliva.

I surge up out of my half sleep, leap to my feet and shed my blankets, all in one brisk movement while attempting to get to Jess as quickly as I can.

I adjust Jess's head position just in time.

Not only was Jess's nose extremely congested but her mouth was filled with saliva.

Guilt-ridden that I was sleeping as Jess was choking, I lay back down on my mattress on the floor, mentally exhausted, paralyzed by the events.

I am emotionally and physically drained, it is as if all of my life has been sucked out of me.

I just can't imagine not being able to communicate when one is in danger.
BettyJane and I have been working with Jess for more than five years, trying to get her to talk again.

As I lay awake, a thought comes to my mind.

If Jess were able to talk – what would she say?

I have never had another panic attack after my snorkeling episode ever again in my life.
That is, up until now.
Fear rises up my chest and starts to control me; it starts to burn my house down as I realize that all of this time I had never taken into consideration what Jess might actually want.

"How could anyone want to live this way, for this long?"
What would Jess request if she could communicate with me right now?

What if Jess was able to talk and her first two words were:

"*Mo Cushlie?*"

That disturbing thought is interrupted by Jess coughing.

She coughs so violently that a pillow falls off of her bed.

I bend over and pick it up with both hands.

I have one hand on each end of the pillow.

As I am standing up to put the pillow back on her bed, my prior thought reenters my mind...

"Mo Cushlie."

I half entertain the thought.

I would definitely trade my freedom in society for Jess's freedom from a paralyzed body.
I would definitely go to hell for her to get to heaven.

Her suffering can end.

Just like that.

I slowly pull away and sit down on the couch in the dark.

I play the thought out in my mind.

I can see myself calling the police.

I can see myself openly confessing to the act of mercy.

I can see the handcuffs.

I can see the trial.

I can see the verdict.

I can see the jail cell.

I can see myself in it.

None of this stops me.

What stops me are my fathers' words before he disappeared from my dream:

"Do what you want to do, John.

Trust yourself."

So I trust myself in my belief that if Jess were able to talk, she would say she would want to live.

She would want to fight.

She would want to continue to experience life as long as she was with her family, surrounded by love.

"John, there is going to be a time in your life when you are going to be in the fight of your life, and that's how I want you to fight."

What stops me is what I cannot see.

What stops me is the photo of my father, the acorn and me.

Actually, just of the acorn and me.

My father is not there.

I remember how that made me feel.

What stops me is my realization that when my family reunites, whole in the future, to take that family photo that will last for eternity, I would not be in it.

It is then I realize my job is not to put an end to the suffering, but rather to find meaning in the suffering.

To plant the seed of a greater good.

I put the pillow down.

I let the fear subside down my chest, and the thought vanishes.

It never resurfaces again.

"Fire can either burn your house down or heat your house; it is all whether it controls you, or you control it."

Near the end of your souls' journey, all of the lessons you have learned along the way will be tested to see if they are galvanized enough to withstand true battle.

Cynthia Occelli wrote:
"For a seed to achieve its greatest expression, it must come completely undone.

The shell cracks, its insides come out, and everything changes.
To someone who doesn't understand growth, it would look like complete destruction."

Unless you have absolutely had enough and want to quit, then you haven't given it your all.

Because it is after you momentarily quit and you reverse the course that you gain your greatest momentum...

Before I go back to sleep, I give the dark side of my soul some advice:

"You should give up, trying to make me give up."

- 25 -
DON'T EAT MY FOOD

The first and final thing
That you have to do in this world,
Is to last it
And not be smashed by it.

Ernest Hemingway

My most important win, and my only win, as a college wrestler, did not occur in a gym on a wrestling mat, it occurred off campus, on my kitchen floor.

It was the fall of 1983; I was a freshman at college.

My father was out of work for a couple of years before I went off to college.

Money was tight, real tight.

When my parents dropped me off at Southern Connecticut University and handed me a bag of food, it was understood that bag of food needed to last for a while.

There was no meal plan.
My meal plan *was* that bag of food.

A bag, which on the first night in the house I left unprotected.

To my dismay, when I awoke the next morning, my food was gone.

I made the mistake of asking my new roommates, "Who ate my food?" in front of everybody.

And of course, it was the wrestler who weighed 220 pounds.

Remember, back then I only weighed 126 pounds.

I said, "Listen, all you had to do was ask, I would have let you have some of my food."

He said, "Nah, it doesn't work that way."

I said, "What?"

He said: "It doesn't work that way. I will eat your food whenever I want to eat your food."

To galvanize his point that he could do whatever he wanted, without any fear of retribution, he swatted my head as he walked by me.

He then made the mistake of turning his back on me and dismissing me.

As soon as he turned his back on me, I lowered my shoulder, and I rammed it into the small of his back.

He fell, face first, to the ground.

I knew what was coming next.
He got up, and he beat the heck out of me for a few minutes.

He continued to do this until he thought he got his point across. The point is that he was going to eat my food, and there was nothing that I could do or say was going to stop him from doing so.

He eventually got up, turned around and started to walk away thinking he was victorious.

I also got back up, and I rammed my lower shoulder into the small of his back again.

And the process repeated itself for a few more minutes - he beats the heck out of me, I get up, he turns his back on me, and I ram my shoulder into the small of his back, and he falls, face first, onto the floor.

On about the sixth cycle of this process, he decided he needed to teach me a lesson.

As I was approaching to annoyingly put my shoulder into the small of his back for the sixth time, he turned around and viciously head locked me. My feet flew above my head and on the way down they landed on the edge of the kitchen table with such force I thought I had broken my leg. I had never experienced such pain in my life. I mean the pain just shot through my body almost pleading with me, begging me to stop getting back up, to just lay there.

Which, I did.

As my oxygen was being cut off by his intense vice grip on my head, I played possum.
I played dead.

I made believe I submitted.
It was the only way out.

And it worked.

He not so gingerly got off me and walked away.

He never even considered looking over his shoulders to see if I was going to attack him a seventh time.

That was a mistake on his part.

This time I allowed him to get a few feet further away from me so I could get a running start, then I rammed my shoulder into the small of his back again for the seventh time.

With the running start, I was able to build up enough force to jackknife his back when I exploded into him.

This time I was quick to my feet and was able to get away from his grasp when I said to him, "I don't care what you do to me. You are not going to eat my food unless I give you permission."

I didn't care about the consequences. I could take any physical beating. He was nearly one hundred pounds heavier than I, it only made sense that he could physically dominate me.

I knew he was going to beat the heck out of me until he felt I was going to stay down on my own, so his power over me would continue without his body having to physically be on top of me, keeping me down.

But I wasn't going to let him mentally dominate me.

That I could control.

At this point, he had a decision to make. He either could never turn his back on me again or go away and decide it was not worth his effort.

He confused having physical dominance over me with having mental dominance over me.

He may have physically outweighed me by one hundred pounds, but mentally he was no match for me.

I was going to get up and fight every time I got knocked down.

No matter what physical beating he laid on me, he was never going to get to my will.

He realized the same thing. He turned to me and said, "You're crazy man, it's just not worth it."

And he called a truce.

Life is the same way.

Some events will absolutely dominate you in life, but you can never let them seep into your soul and break your will.
Belief, confidence, enthusiasm, optimism, hope, these traits you need to protect like a kings treasure, for they are more valuable than any currency in life.

There are days life is going to try to eat your food.

And the honest truth is, it can.

You only have two choices.

The first being, to sit back, let it happen and let your will be broken.

And the other is to fight back, knowing you are going to take a beating, but your will and soul will remain whole.

Always fight back.

The beatings stop, and the wounds will heal.

Broken wills, seldom do.

Hearns taught me that night in 1985 that you don't even have to win the fight to be considered a winner. Sometimes giving it all you have is enough.

Every time you get up and fight, it takes the fun out of it for life.

All life wants is to know you will stay down without it having to be there, keeping you down.

Once it realizes your will is strong and you will get up every time it knocks you down, it will move on because it can't accomplish what it set out to do.

And that is to dominate your soul.

Which you, and only you alone, control.

Eventually, life will just move on to something else.

And your soul will flourish.

- 26 -
3 A.M. Emails

As we express our gratitude,
We must never forget
The highest appreciation
Is not to utter words,
But to live by them.

John F. Kennedy

I play the lottery by online subscription because it is my way of making sure if I win, I would automatically be notified of it.

A yearly subscription costs $2 a week or $104 a year.

It is the best $104 I have ever invested, even if I never win the grand prize.

That is because every once in a while I will get an email from NY State Lottery with the headline, **"NY Lottery Subscription Prize Notification,"** and for that brief moment I am filled with endless possibility.

This email always comes when I need it the most - when my mind is stuck in what Zig Ziglar would call some "Stinkin Thinking."

Every one of the emails I have received over the years having the subject as, "NY Lottery Subscription Prize Notification" has always been a notification I had won only $1 or $2.

That $1 or $2 notification winning, though, was invaluable.

For that brief second, before I open the email, endless possibilities existed.

Writing "6 Minutes Wrestling with Life," has been very cathartic for me, and has been my online subscription to love, hope and possibility.

It is funny how I came about knowing I should write the book.

Back in 2012, Yolanda Vega appeared on my TV to pull the Lottery numbers.

My wife was in the other room - so I yelled out:

"Here are my numbers for tonight's Lottery:

9, 7, 6, 12.

Numbers that I didn't play.
I started to say my 6 numbers thinking that it was Lotto...

After I yelled out my first four numbers the first ball went up the shoot:
9
"Wow, that's weird."

The second ball goes up the shoot, 7.

"You got to be kidding me."

I yell out to BettyJane, "Come here fast;" she does, but she thinks I am playing a joke on her, that I somehow already know the numbers because I delayed the broadcast.

I did not.

The third ball - 6.

"Please don't do this to me," was my first thought...

I have a momentary relief when I realize the drawing is not for Lotto, it is for the Pick 4 and Pick 3 drawings. Even if I did predict the numbers and did not play them that it wouldn't be a missed life-changing event.

Fourth Ball - 1.

"Wow, that makes me feel a little better."

"Now for the pick 3 numbers," I hear from the TV. "First ball – 2."

The chill goes through my body as I just realized that I, on the spur of the moment, just picked 9 7 6 12 as my numbers and the first 5 numbers that went up the shoot were 9 7 6 1 2.

I looked at BettyJane - she is still 50/50 on whether she thinks I am pulling one over on her.

I convince her that I'm not.
She bluntly says to me, *"You get nothing if it's not on paper."*

A few hours go by and then it dawns on me that I may not have won the lotto, but I may have just received something even more valuable.

I tapped into my soul, and I just got my answer.

You see, inside my head for the longest time, I had wanted to write.

I always knew since I was six years of age that I would write.

I know now, it is time.

Most people would be angry that they got nothing for picking five numbers.

I look at it as getting my answer.
Write.

"You get nothing if it's not on paper."

Every once in a while I receive an email from someone who has just read "6 Minutes Wrestling With Life." They share with me their life's experiences and let me know I have touched their soul in some small way.

These correspondences always rejuvenate me.

They touch my soul.

I have always said the absolute greatest part of writing my book "6 Minutes Wrestling With Life" has been the people I have met. The people who reached out and shared their lives with me.

These inspiring emails always seem to appear exactly when I need them the most, often, in the middle of a hard night of caregiving, around 3 am.

Hence, I call them my 3 am emails.

Inspiring messages sent to me when I need them the most.

Every 3 am email I have ever received has had the timely precision of an engineer.

I have learned to pay attention to every late night correspondence I receive.

I believe they were sent for a very distinct reason.

I believe within them there is something I need to know, or to learn, or to have my belief reignited, or have my confidence confirmed, or my enthusiasm renewed.

I value them deeply.
Tonight's 3 a.m. email is no different.

It is amazing how these late night emails are so inspiring.

And arrive precisely when my energy level falls below "E."

I likened them to when I was driving to Pittsburg a few years back, and I inadvertently let the gas run low really low.

So I use my GPS to find the nearest gas station.

The nearest gas station was 28 miles away.
I had no more than 5 miles left at most.

That posed a problem.

The only solution was to drive towards the gas station 28 miles away, knowing that I was probably going to run out of gas and would have to walk a very long way, alone, in the dark.

Four miles into my plan, I saw this beautiful sign that said, "Grand Opening - Refuel Here."

A gas station so new, it was not on the GPS yet.

I drove into the station on fumes.

And I refueled.

Just in time.

These 3 a.m. emails are my "Grand Opening" inspirational gas stations.

An inspirational gassing station that appears out of nowhere to refuel my soul.

A 3 a.m. email arrives tonight from a US Marine having a hard time returning to civilian life.

He says the letters I arranged into words on a piece of paper have somehow helped him in his life.

As he states, and I also believe,

"There are no coincidences in life, just signs of divine confirmation that we are on the right path on each of our own unique journeys."

"These signs are always there, and if we're not seeing them, it's simply because we're not looking, because we lost belief," he goes on to say.

He says, *"My life has been missing meaning,"* as he puts it, *"I have been trying to catch air,"* and he hasn't yet been able to do so.

He says through my book he has found gratitude, the one thing he has lacked in his life.

I read that line again.

Imagine - a US Marine thanking me for gratitude.

No Sir - I am the grateful one.

Thank you.

These 3 a.m. emails always come when I need them the most.

I now realize the real meaning of "You get nothing if it's not on paper," refers not to the riches of winning the lottery, but to the riches of tapping into the human spirit.

"You get nothing if it's not on paper."

I have met such wonderful people on this journey and each of them in their own unique way has made me spiritually richer.

I would have run out of gas long ago if it were not for the gas stations that appeared out of nowhere filling my spiritual gas tank, throughout my unique journey.

- 27 -

THUMPER

We've got to tell everybody.
We've got to remind them.
We've got to remind them how good it is.
People have forgotten what life is all about.
They've forgotten what it is to be alive.
They need to be reminded
Of what they have and what they can lose.
What I feel is the joy of life,
The gift of life,
The freedom of life,
The wonderment of life!

Leonard Lowe
Awakenings

A few years ago our neighbors that lived across the street foreclosed on their home, they upped and left in the middle of the night leaving everything they owned behind, including their two cats.
Those two cats soon became four cats, then eight cats, and then sixteen.

I have found healing qualities by writing.
BettyJane has found healing qualities by nurturing these cats back to life, feeding them and sheltering them from harsh winters and eventually finding permanent homes for them.

Over the last few years, she has found a loving home for over forty-four cats.

She is very good at it; she cares a great deal for them and has had some miraculous saves.

I can recall more than a few kittens she hand fed with a baby's bottle because their own mother abandoned them; kittens who were only hours away from death that she invigorated and nurtured back to life.

It is a bittersweet feeling for her when she hands over a kitten to their new family.

Even with finding homes for over forty-four cats, there is one cat she could never give away.

That was Thumper.

The sun comes up, and I walk into my kitchen for a drink of water.

There, somewhere equidistant between the floor and the ceiling, hanging on to the screen on my screen door with his claws is Thumper.

A smile immediately forms on my face.

That's what Thumper does, every time you see him, he makes you smile.

He makes you smile while he is doing absolutely nothing.

He is sort of the Seinfeld of cats.

I can watch him all day chase his shadow, play with a ball, roll in the grass or lie on his back taking in the sun.

He exudes awe and wonderment in everything he does.

Nothing is ordinary to him.

Thumper is lying on the porch.

My initial reaction is that he is sunbathing again.

He is not.

He is dead.

Lying beside Thumper is a half eaten mouse.

A mouse that recently ate the poison that a neighbor put down to end his existence.

The mouse ate the poison; Thumper ate the mouse.

Thumper is gone.

Why did the Universe take a soul who provided such happiness to the world?

I don't have access to those parts of the Universe's plan, but I believe a better question is, "Why did the Universe put Thumper in our lives?"

And that question I can answer.

The Universe put Thumper in our lives for us to learn to have an enthusiasm for life, to find awe in our life, to cherish life's most ordinary moments.

I do know there are Thumpers throughout all of our lives, people who come into our life at the exact moment we need them.

They do their job, and then they move on.

Thumper showed a zeal for life.

He made ordinary, extraordinary.

That is exactly what my life needed to see.

Every time I think of Thumper hanging by his claws half way up my screen door, I smile.

I smile at the wonderment of life.

- 28 -

BLESS YOU

The range of what we see and do
Is limited by what we fail to notice.
And because we fail to notice
That we fail to notice,
There is little we can do
To change
Until we notice
How failing to notice
Shapes our thoughts and deeds.

R. D. Laing

In everything you do, you are either moving towards or away from your goal.

That is why at 3:18 a.m. I am heading up the stairs to my bedroom where my wife sleeps alone.

I enter the room, and I approach her.

"BettyJane."
 "BettyJane," I say again, this time while lightly shaking her arm to wake her.

"WHAT, WHAT IS IT – IS JESS OK?" BettyJane alarmingly asks.

"Jess is fine."

"Then what?"

"I just wanted to say 'Bless you.'"

"What?"

"You sneezed today, I heard it, and I didn't say 'Bless you.'"

"You woke me up in the middle of the night to say 'bless you' to me?"

"Yes, I was lying awake, going over the whole day in my mind and I realized earlier when you sneezed, I heard you sneeze and I didn't say 'Bless you.'

That is not how I want to live – I never want to take you or our lives for granted.

All we have is each other, and the time we spend with one another.

It is so easy to overlook the small things in our lives, but it is the small things that turn into the big things.

So I didn't want a bad small thing to get started, so I decided to wake you up and say, "Bless you," so I can stop it from getting any bigger."

"Thank you – now get out of here - I have to get up in two hours."

I have spent my whole life trying to be extraordinary and in the process overlooking the magnificence in the ordinary.

I have come to realize one of the most extraordinary things in this world is for one to appreciate the ordinary.

The magnificence of an ordinary day.

In an ordinary year.

With an ordinary person.

The other day, while I was driving with my son from New York to New Jersey, I realized how much magnificence we take for granted each day.

As I approached the toll booth, which read, "Toll $12," I started to complain to myself about the cost. Then I caught myself when I realized for $12 there was a bridge that was going to allow my son and me to travel safely over a mile of water in less than one minute.

That while I was driving, my iPhone was talking to me, giving me directions to my intended destination.

If I made a wrong turn, the same iPhone would quickly correct my course with new directions.

And while I was driving over the bridge, my son was watching a movie on his iPad, which he held in his hand.

That ordinary, to me, is extraordinary.

One of the keys to happiness is to see what others overlook and take for granted.

Appreciation and gratitude are powerful fuels.

They allow you to be in the moment.

What dying person does not crave for just one more moment of an ordinary day, in an ordinary year, with an ordinary person?

When you really think about it, one's ability to realize that the ordinary days probably outnumber the extraordinary days 750 to 1.

One's happiness and ability to make the ordinary days amazing is very important to one's life.

I contest the average person only remembers about 50 days in their life, their wedding day, the birth of their kids, the loss of a loved one, etc.
If one were to live to be 100, one would have lived 36,500 days.

Imagine if you only remembered the special days that would leave 36,450 ordinary days, unremembered.

The quality of ones' life is in direct proportion to their ability to be amazed by the ordinary.

I contest ones' ability to make the ordinary, extraordinary is much more important than having a few memorable days.

There is so much to be in awe of in life.

If one realizes that the ordinary is extraordinary one will always be happy.

Ralph Waldo Emerson said:
"If the stars were to appear but one night every thousand years how man would marvel and adore."

Adore the stars, may you be able to see them shine in the light as well as in the dark.

- 29 -
THE VOICE

Once you have tasted flight,
You will forever walk the earth
With your eyes turned skyward,
For there you have been,
And there you will always long to return.

Leonardo Da Vinci

February 18th, 2015

"Hi"

Just two letters.

Two letters strung together with so much might.

Two letters said to two visiting friends.

"Hi."

Just one word.

One word that has more meaning than any book that has ever been written, any language that has ever been spoken.
"Hi," in Jessie's voice, a voice that I almost forgot.

The voice that turned everyone's chairs around.

The voice that made our collective souls sing.

A voice uttered from a smiling mouth with a look that said,

"I am thankful that I am alive, among family and friends whom I know love me."

It took nearly six years for Jess to send a message from her brain to her mouth, to our ears, into our hearts.

Just two letters.

Two letters that mean the world to my family.

Two letters that went into our ears as love and came out of our eyes as tears.

"You are so there," I believe was Jess's friend's shocked reaction...

Yes, she is.

The bamboo seed has finally made its way through the soil.

- 30 -

THE FOREST FOR THE TREES

*The creation of one thousand forests
Is in one acorn.*

Ralph Waldo Emerson

"Do what you want to do John.

Trust yourself."

Thank you, Dad.

I will see you when it is time for that family photo.

Until then Dad, be well.

In my mind's eye, my father's image appears in the photo I took with him in my dream.

Sometimes in life, you just need time to allow the full picture to develop.

The seed of something greater.

One thousand forests.

All from one acorn.

Thank you for reading

"Your Soul Knows"

JohnA Passaro

CONTACT AND AUTHOR INFO
3 A.M. EMAILS

The greatest benefit I have received from my writing are the people who have reached out to me and have shared their life stories with me.

I cherish every email I receive.

I encourage you to contact me.

Email - johnapassaro@icloud.com

Like me on Facebook - www.facebook.com/john.passaro.50

Follow me on Twitter - @johnapassaro

Blog – www.johnapassaroblog.com

COULD I ASK YOU FOR A FAVOR?

The greatest compliment that a reader can pay a writer is to tell a friend about their book.

I would be honored if you were able to do so.

WORD OF MOUTH
The simplest way to find great books to read is when friends share their reading experiences with each other by word of mouth.

BOOK REVIEWS
If you feel this book has touched you in a small way or has stirred emotions inside of you that have given you a different perspective on life, I invite for you to leave a book review on the site that you purchased this book. This will allow potential readers to understand the book is worth the investment of their time and money.

The Book Review doesn't need to be perfect; it just needs to be something from you, letting other readers know how you feel about this book.

SOCIAL MEDIA
Please share your reading experience with your friends on your Facebook and Twitter social media pages.

I thank you in advance, as all communication to your family and friends is greatly appreciated.

ALL BOOKS BY JOHNA PASSARO

SHARING INSPIRATION AND OPTIMISM

A GOOD MAN

WRESTLING WITH LIFE SERIES

6 MINUTES WRESTLING WITH LIFE (BOOK 1)

AGAIN (BOOK 2)

YOUR SOUL KNOWS (BOOK 3)

www.**JOHNAPASSAROBLOG**.com

Made in the USA
Columbia, SC
30 January 2020